S0-BQZ-917

18 TAILOR-MADE
Model Railroad Track Plans

BY JOHN ARMSTRONG

Editor: Bob Hayden
Copy Editor: Marcia Stern
Proofreader: Burr Angle
Art Director: Lawrence Luser
Staff Artist: Bill Scholz

KALMBACH K BOOKS

First printing, 1983. Second printing, 1988.

The cover painting by Chuck Boie shows the scene at Placerville on
the HOn3 Rio Grande Southern layout described on pages 50 through 52.

by John H. Armstrong. All rights reserved. This book may not be reproduced in part or in
without written permission from the publisher, except in the case of brief quotations used
ws. Purchaser may have photocopies of drawings made locally as an aid to building his
railroad layout, but is prohibited from distribution of copies of the drawings to others.
ed by Kalmbach Publishing Co., 1027 North Seventh Street, Milwaukee, WI 53233.
in U. S. A. Library of Congress Catalog Card Number: 83-81463. ISBN: 0-89024-040-X.

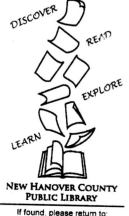
DISCOVER READ EXPLORE LEARN

NEW HANOVER COUNTY
PUBLIC LIBRARY

If found, please return to:
201 Chestnut St.
Wilmington, NC 28401
(910) 798-6300
http://www.nhclibrary.org

NEW HANOVER COUNTY PUBLIC LIBRARY

Givens and druthers in custom railroad planning

Getting at the priorities that influence a tailor-made track plan

TRUTH IS AT LEAST more realistic than fiction, so railroads custom designed to fit actual spaces, real restrictions, and the specific dreams and desires of real model railroaders should represent the greatest challenges to a track planner. In fact, they do. This book is a sampling of 18 such railroads, 18 layouts that I was commissioned to plan during several years in the custom railroad planning business.

The person who designs a lot of track plans has some advantages over the fellow whose only goal is to come up with the one "right" plan for himself. These advantages range from a collection of curve templates (which are considerably more convenient than a compass in working up a drawing accurate enough to be sure that things will really fit) to a certain pessimism as to what can be done in a given area (which saves time in trying dozens of alternatives) to — most important in my case — a permanently plugged-in electric erasing machine. (The latter item allows me to work in ink on tracing paper with the confidence that comes from being able to goof in the same location a few times before wearing a hole all the way through the paper.)

On the other hand, no one other than the prospective layout builder can ever know quite so accurately and vividly just what are those things that are most to be desired in his ultimate railroad. At best, there is bound to be some loss in transmitting these features and concepts from the railroad owner to the "architect," who must endeavor to incorporate them, on paper, into the layout. This is particularly true since neither party can afford to engage in limitless correspondence on the matter.

Nevertheless, there are enough common aspects in designing layouts of almost any size, shape, purpose, or style that a standardized process can do an acceptable job of passing the word. Each of the plans in this book was derived from a standard planning materials package completed by the layout builder.

The available-space diagram. The mechanics of making sure that the layout will fit the space are taken care of by having the railroad owner mark up a diagram of his area on a grid. This diagram is to a scale of ⅜", ¾", or 1½" to the foot, the same scale that the track plan will be drawn to, and includes a checklist of obstacles whose presence and dimensions must be known if trouble is to be avoided later.

Cross sections are included with the available-space diagram if attic ceiling slopes or other overhead items make them necessary. Railroad boundaries

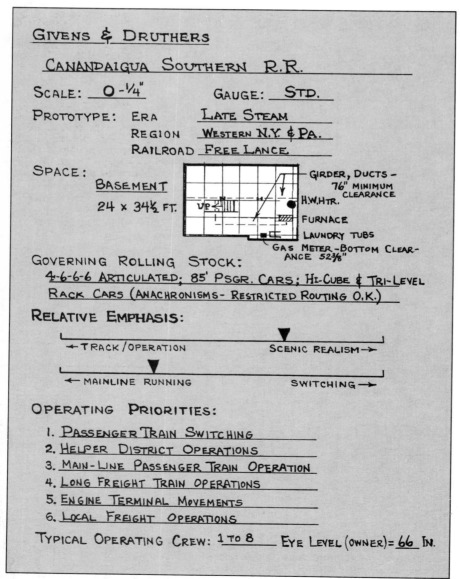

Fig. 1-1 A "GIVENS AND DRUTHERS" SUMMARY

are indicated as being either physical (walls, mostly) or political (other family members, mostly), and the physical or political penetrability of each boundary is also indicated where it could conceivably affect the design. My "guarantee" is that the layout as designed will fit the *drawing* of the space, thus putting the burden of accuracy on the man who wields the tape measure. Since the track plan is made on tracing paper over the diagram furnished by the railroad owner, the likelihood of errors in transcription is minimized.

The questionnaire. The much more complex matter of being reasonably sure that things of first importance are so recognized and given proper attention is attacked with an insultingly prying and lengthy questionnaire. The "Givens and druthers" table included with each track plan in this book is a condensation of the most significant replies in the questionnaire. Figure 1-1 is an example.

Simply reading and filling out the questionnaire and available-space drawing, Fig. 1-2, are of real benefit in clarifying the goals of the railroad owner's layout design, and he often decides at that point that he can go ahead and work out the design for himself. (The other possibilities are that he decides that my help is worth the price, or returns to his favorite armchair to think about it for a few more years.) Since this business of establishing likes and dislikes and priorities among them is so important in developing and understanding the finished plan, it's worth taking time to discuss each factor here.

Governing rolling stock. The effect of rolling stock characteristics on the track plan is fundamental. There are some classes of locomotives or cars which must be able to operate satisfactorily on the railroad, and whether this is a matter of reliability or appearance it determines the minimum radius. This, in turn, allows analyzing the space in terms of "squares," Fig. 1-3, for preliminary planning. (Use of the square in track planning is covered in detail in my earlier book, TRACK PLANNING FOR REALISTIC OPERATION.)

Determining to what degree rolling stock will limit what is possible in the plan is a subjective process: An 1890 Ten-Wheeler that will scoot around an 18″ radius in HO will still look nicer on a 36″ curve — which is also suitable for a Big Boy; the 4-8-8-4 can be worked over (with increasingly severe compromises with regard to strict scale and detailing) to get around 30″ or perhaps even 26″ curves. Of course, the Big Boy will cut a wider and wider swath with its boiler overhang — and look awful in the process — but there may be ways to allow for and hide these problems to the extent that, overall, the railroad with the tighter curves is still preferable.

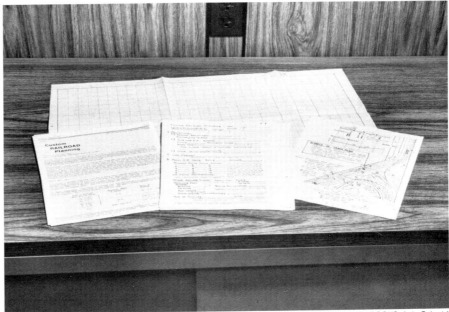

KALMBACH BOOKS: A. L. Schmidt

Fig. 1-2. Each of the 18 plans in this book was developed from a standard planning materials package similar to this one. The package consists of a four-page questionnaire and a blank drawing form for recording dimensions and obstacles in the layout space.

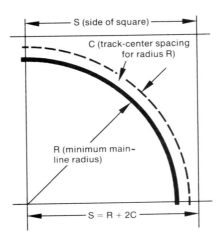

Fig. 1-3 WHAT IS A TRACK-PLANNING SQUARE, AND HOW BIG IS IT?

The key dimension in any track plan is the minimum radius of the main line. This, plus the minimum track-center spacing, determines the size of the track-planning square. The side dimension of the square is equal to the minimum mainline radius plus two times the minimum track-center spacing.

TYPICAL SQUARE SIZES		N	HO	O
SHARP CURVES	Min. radius	10″	18″	33″
Suitable for four-axle diesels, 40-foot freight cars	2X track-center spacing	2 × 1¼″	2 × 2″	2 × 4″
	Square size	12½″	22″	41″
CONVENTIONAL CURVES	Min. radius	13″	24″	43½″
All diesels, 2-8-2s, and shorty passenger cars operate well and don't look too repulsive	2X track-center spacing	2 × 1¼″	2 × 2″	2 × 4″
	Square size	15½″	28″	51½″
BROAD CURVES	Min. radius	16½″	30″	54″
Will handle all equipment with normal modifications and good, if not great, appearance	2X track-center spacing	2 × 1¼″	2 × 2″	2 × 4″
	Square size	19″	34″	62″
SUPER-BROAD CURVES	Min. radius	19½″	36″	66″
Will handle all equipment easily with much better appearance	2X track-center spacing	2 × 1¼″	2 × 2″	2 × 4″
	Square size	22″	40″	74″

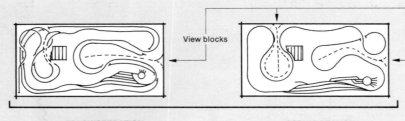

TRACK/OPERATION

A mark on the scale toward track and operation means including view blocks to divide the railroad wherever there's room, but not at the expense of going around the space twice to get a really long mainline run.

SCENIC REALISM

A mark toward scenic realism means that only a single segment of the main line should be in view at any one point, except where there might be a loop on the prototype railroad.

Fig. 1-4 TRACK AND OPERATION VERSUS SCENIC REALISM

Governing rolling stock, then, is a point on which there may have to be some compromise. As a result the size of the track-planning squares in the finished plans may not have been that used for the first-cut look at what *might* fit. Sometimes a single piece of equipment which is grossly more demanding in this respect, though a favorite, may end up as a shelf model in favor of compromising the entire track plan. More often it is possible to balance things by providing a limited operating territory for the one problem child while taking advantage of the curving capabilities of the rest of the roster in designing other segments of the railroad.

Track versus scenery. All our model railroads are overcrowded with track — the differences are only matters of degree — so the questionnaire asks the railroad owner to position an arrowhead on a linear scale between the extremes of track/operation (track at any price) and scenic realism (relatively uncluttered scenes). Although the scale is continuous there's a fairly distinct watershed here: A mark toward the left end means the owner will accept multiple laps of track passing through the scene to provide a long main line, while the man who draws his arrow near the right margin will insist on staying away from *visible* spaghetti-bowl tendencies by allowing only one segment of main line in any scene, Fig. 1-4.

A similar relative-emphasis scale

helps in selecting a schematic arrangement for the railroad. A mark to the left, calling for lots of mainline running, usually means either a continuous-run or loop-to-loop plan; one way over at the right calls for a point-to-point line that requires breaking up and reassembling consists after each trip; and an arrowhead near the middle often means that a stub-terminal, out-and-back layout is indicated, Fig. 1-5.

Operating priorities. Next comes the matter of operating priorities, and the smaller the railroad, the more important it is to put first things first. This means limiting the variety of railroading portrayed so that the train movements that are represented are of enough scope to be worthwhile. The questionnaire lists ten types of operation which the railroad owner is to rank in numerical priority, crossing out those of no interest.

The exact order of the top few priorities isn't all that crucial in a pike that's large enough to do several things reasonably well, and no one's exact ranking is cast in concrete, anyway. On an evening when you feel like watching the long freight trains run, their real priority is high, and should some manufacturer bring out an irresistible series of kits for all the components of a late-steam-era engine servicing facility, the desirability of allowing room for a steady procession of movements of your brass locomotives beneath the coal dock, on and off the turntable, in and out of the roundhouse, and back

and forth to road assignments would certainly move upward a notch or two.

What are the typical priorities of typical model railroaders? Magazine editors have always had to make assumptions in this regard, whether in picking articles on the basis of likely appeal to a broad spectrum of readers or in seeking to nudge the hobby as a whole in what they considered "healthy" directions. Manufacturers likewise have an interest in trying to predict what items will sell — recognizing, of course, that model railroaders who actually run trains are probably not the big end of the market compared to the collectors and modelbuilders whose support makes the whole hobby financially and technically practical these days.

Results from an unscientific survey. Recognizing again that those far enough into the hobby to be willing to pay for track planning on a custom basis (and put up with the nuisance of completing a nosy questionnaire) aren't necessarily "typical," Fig. 1-6 summarizes all questionnaire responses on operating priorities to date (not just the 18-plan sampling in this book).

While the choices available on the questionnaire undoubtedly influence the results (for example, there's no provision for expressing a preference for traction operation), it's apparent that freight comes first and the role of the local freight in feeding through traffic is well appreciated. If a separate item for freight train switching as distinct from local freight train operations were called out, there is no doubt that it, too, would rank high.

Passenger trains are a lot more popular than I'd expected, and passenger train switching shows up as of considerably broader interest than the attention given it in the literature to date might indicate. Since commuter service in recent years has been restricted to a few urban areas, it's not surprising that there is little general interest in modeling it, but several who did rate it put it at the top of their priorities.

Time factors — two kinds. Another dimension in modeling is time — operating the layout in accordance with a schedule, with or without the distance-stretching factor of a fast clock. So far, timetable operation is not one of the desired factors for most model railroaders, but there are a few for which it approaches top priority, usually coupled with a willingness to wrap a long main line with many short sidings into the available area to thoroughly challenge engineers and dispatchers. Looking forward to computerization, there is more than occasional interest in timetable operation for one-man railroading.

On the historical time scale the ability to turn back the clock is almost universally appreciated, but the knob practically stops cold at one specific point: More than 85 percent of all custom

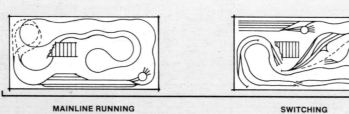

MAINLINE RUNNING

A mark on the scale toward mainline running means a loop-to-loop or continuous main line and probably only one principal yard at which some (but not all) consists are switched.

SWITCHING

A mark toward switching calls for a true point-to-point schematic, requiring a full halt and rearrangement of the consist for the next trip. Branches are also common.

Fig. 1-5 MAINLINE RUNNING VERSUS SWITCHING

pikes to date include railroading in the late-steam era! Even the numerous narrow gaugers seem to prefer modeling the latter-day East Broad Top, Rio Grande, or SP "Slim Princess" to the same lines set in earlier times, Fig. 1-7.

Spreading the railroading era modeled over a few decades by running locomotives and cars of different generations at different times — or at the same time, accepting some degree of anachronism — is popular, with many late-steam-era fans planning to allow GP40s, high-cubes, and tank hoppers on the property. On the other hand, less than 10 percent are willing to stick strictly to post-steam operations.

When it comes to basing a model railroad on a specific period earlier than late-steam, only the turn of the century has attracted a significant following. Setting a model railroad in this era is both practical and space-saving; you retain the practical advantages of automatic couplers and reasonably accommodating boiler and firebox dimensions, while gaining the space-saving characteristics of significantly shorter freight and passenger cars, locomotives that fit on short turntables and look good on modest curves, and no tall cars that require extra vertical clearance (and as a result, stiffer grades) over the whole track plan.

Are there many others modeling Civil War railroading, the gravity lines of Pennsylvania and their connections, or, for that matter, pre-super-power

WHAT ARE THE PRIORITIES?

	Weighted* priority	Breadth of interest**
Medium-length freight-train operations (10-15 cars)	100	75%
Local freight operations	87	81%
Mainline passenger-train operations (8-12 cars)	72	59%
Branchline or short passenger trains (3-4 cars)	70	63%
Engine terminal movements	61	84%
Long freight-train operations (more than 20 cars)	50	56%
Helper-district operations	45	59%
Passenger-train switching (station/terminal)	43	56%
Timetable operation (fast clock)	32	41%
Commuter trains/traffic	16	22%

* First priority = 10, second = 8, third = 6, fourth = 5, fifth = 4, sixth = 3, seventh = 2, eighth = 1

** Percent including item on desired list

Fig. 1-6 WHAT ARE THE PRIORITIES?

mainline operations of the early 1920s? No indication of it so far, but remember who's included in the sample. I consider it highly likely that anyone dedicating himself to such an off-the-beaten-track era would research the railroad operations and the wayside scenes of his period so thoroughly that he'd need no further assistance in coming up with a suitable track plan.

Working buildings into the priorities. A separate question, but one related to both operating priorities and the era modeled, inquires about structures to be worked into the plan. These range from so specific an item as the

Pittsburgh & Lake Erie's grand old station alongside the Monongahela River at Smithfield Street, Pittsburgh, to unidentified representatives of a class of building such as the small-town business block. Bridges are such fascinatingly detailed and impressive items that some modelers give them a high enough priority to ensure a place for one or two really big ones, letting the rest of the track plan be subordinated to their space requirements, Fig. 1-8.

If structures and modeling them are a big part of the hobby for the man ordering up the custom layout, track shouldn't be allowed to crowd them out

Robert Hale

Fig. 1-7. The most popular period among those model railroaders commissioning custom plans, bar none, is the late-steam era, which allows the modeler to combine steam and die-sel power on the layout. This 1952 Union Pacific scene at Cajon Pass, California, includes the kind of action called for in many of the tailor-made plans presented in this book.

Collection of Edward H. Meyers

Fig. 1-8. A spectacular bridge can set the theme for a tailor-made plan. The Kate Shelley viaduct that carries the Chicago & North Western over the Des Moines River near Boone, Iowa, is such a bridge, and the C&NW track plan in this book was designed to incorporate a condensed model of it.

Height is a different matter. The questionnaire asks specifically about the owner's height and limberness (the latter is multiple choice: either "limber" or "not so limber") and both are strongly considered in the design.

On the basis of replies to date, the average height of layout builders is 70.64 inches, with a standard deviation of 2.83 inches. In practical terms this means that two-thirds of them can be expected to stand between 5' 7¾" and 6' 1½" tall.

Some 87.2 percent consider themselves limber, but a few qualify this with a "so far" or suggest that planning ahead for a less-completely limber future might be a good idea. Fortunately, I have always been able to come up with no-stoop track plans for the "not so limber" minority.

What about club railroads, where presumably there is a spectrum of heights to be respected in settling altitude questions? So far, this consideration has been academic — the clubs who came to me for a custom track plan have disbanded before their jobs worked their way up through my backlog! Each of the plans in this book was designed to suit its individual owner's stature best. Shorter operators or visitors can be built up toward standard height with clogs; taller ones can learn to duck a little extra!

Other matters of height. Sometimes the owner's physique is a secondary consideration. The cheese is particularly binding in the case of attics, where sloping ceilings force choices between usable area on the one hand and height and comfort on the other. Furnace pipes, gas meters, and laundry equipment often pose similar challenges in basements.

In other cases, such as railroading in a spare room, the choice of exact layout height is entirely up to the builder, and the track elevations shown on the plan are representative of my feeling that you're a lot more likely to build a layout too low than too high.

From the scenic-treatment standpoint, of course, it's eye level that counts. While there may be some exceptionally high-browed or low-browed people in the fraternity, for all practical purposes subtracting six inches from your height will provide this figure. I've listed it that way in each "Givens and druthers" table.

The railroad owner sends the completed questionnaire and the available-space diagram to me, and in return all he gets right away is an estimate of the backlog situation — how long it will be before I can realistically expect to start work on his plan. When I do start (months, even years, later) the first task is to determine what's possible in the space, based on all those givens and druthers. This feasibility study is the subject of Chapter Two.

of the picture. This usually means an arrowhead more to the right on the track and operation versus scenic realism scale, but not always. Structures may also be favored by a plan in which a lot of the track necessary for realistic operation is hidden by buildings in front of it or by being relegated to a lower level with "air rights" above to provide real estate for buildings and their surroundings.

In other situations, structures may be space-savers. The vertical sides of commercial buildings and the retaining walls supporting them can do wonders in separating tracks that would otherwise be obviously too close together. Especially in prairie country where we have to crowd in our main lines without the aid of mountains being a structures fan can be an absolute lifesaver.

Fitting the railroad to its owner. Then there's the matter of tailoring the railroad not only to the space but to its owner — after all, one of the bonuses of any hobby is to be able to have some area of your life in which things are done *your* way. Who would miss the

chance to make something as intricate as a transportation system reflect the way he wants things to be in the best of all possible worlds!

Factors such as ocular acuity and the relative importance of sight and sound tend to be taken care of when the owner indicates his scale and gauge — "time and eyeballs fight on the side of the larger scales" — and anyone who is really turned on by the clump-clump-clump of individual axles coming off a turntable isn't about to be satisfied with 1/160 modeling.

Layout height is the principal matter influenced by owner's physique, although access-related items such as comfortable aisle widths and practical lengths of reach also rate consideration. Just as no discreet person would think of asking a doctor's cocktail-party opinion regarding the doctor's own weight problem, so our discreet questionnaire elicits aisle-width criteria based on exceptional girth only in connection with "the dimensions or other characteristics of *friends* who might be involved in the operation of the completed railroad."

What will fit?

A realistic — but Scottish — estimate of how much
material can be worked into a tailor-made plan

AS A SCOTTISH TARTAN merchant of the old school once stated to a friend of mine who was trying in vain to buy a quarter yard more material than the Scot had declared sufficient to make an outfit of a certain size, "A good seamstress doesna' waste cloth." When Dick returned home from his business trip to Edinburgh his wife had to measure three times and check the pattern match at each seam five times before nervously making that first cut.

The objective of model railroad planning is not to cram every last possible inch of track into the available space, nor is it to force everyone in the household to huddle in corners so that the monster may have utterly free rein in expanding throughout the premises. However, given a reasonable space available (without unduly disrupting domestic tranquility, mortgaging the future to acquire an oversize estate, or undertaking an excavation project rivaling the Panama Canal) there will almost always be more railroad to be accommodated than will fit easily.

So, although it is often better to leave certain areas track-free in the interest of more realistic scenes, better-operating main lines, or layouts that are more fun to build and operate because you can do so without painful gymnastics, the plan that "doesna' waste space" unnecessarily will do a better job overall, however cramped or liberal its territorial limits may be. Those eight inches saved at one end by lapping one loop over another where there is no reason for the lower track to be visible may make room for six more cars in the main yard, or let you extend a tangent section at the far end of the railroad to avoid a marginal S-curve situation.

How big is big enough? Usually the space available is pretty well determined in advance by circumstances beyond the railroad owner's control, but occasionally things are more flexible. Perhaps there's money to build a bigger room, time to search for a house with a better basement-to-cost ratio, or some effective means to persuade (or bribe) the rest of the family to accept allocating more area within the exist-

ing boundaries to the railroad. In either case some idea of how big is big enough can be helpful.

Figure 2-1 summarizes the major characteristics of 30 tailor-made track plans (including the 18 in this book) in terms of size. The biggest covers 68 times as many square feet as the smallest, so there's quite a range — you're not likely to be considering a railroad that falls outside the limits.

To put things in terms adaptable to any scale, the size of each plan has been expressed in terms of the mainline minimum radius. If you are thinking of a particular scale and a general class of equipment — an HO railroad whose largest locomotive will be a heavy 2-8-2, say — you have already begun to tie down your curvature. This radius — about 24" in our example — can be translated into the size of a "square" as explained back in Chapter 1, allowing you to evaluate your available area versus your railroading aspirations in terms of a somewhat absurd unit of measure, the "square square."

For our 24"-radius example the corresponding square square would be 28 inches on a side or 784 square inches, which I'm sure doesn't grab you as something that's going to suddenly make everything crystal clear. That's 5.44 square feet, which probably isn't much more meaningful, but is easily translated in these days of the pocket calculator. A 10 x 13-foot room works out to about 24 square squares, and now you can look at Fig. 2-1 and see that this is a size represented by several examples in the mid-20s range.

Allowing for aisles. What about allowing for aisles and such — do you just count the railroad area? Figure 2-2 shows the arbitrary way in which areas have been rated. Where the railroad fills its space out to the walls, with access via walk-in aisles or perhaps a central operating area, the whole area is counted (rounding off the fractions shamelessly), but in the case of island pikes a couple of feet are added on all sides to allow for working room around the layout. Suitable deductions are made for obstacles which cannot (practically) be surrounded by track, and for

facilities such as laundries for which routine, reasonably convenient access must be provided.

Now we have the wherewithal to better appreciate how overall railroad size affects the end product. It's not a precise calculation, of course — the *shape* of any room affects its usability considerably, with an oblong space usually being kinder in accommodating major yards and other nice things than a square room of the same area. Generally, though, each of the more desirable features of a "dream" layout requires a certain minimum space, and Fig. 2-3 shows the approximate point at which each can enter the picture.

Because my fee schedule for custom planning includes a substantial base charge plus a charge per unit of net layout area (this is higher in the smaller scales where there are more tracks to be planned and drawn in each square foot), our sampling probably leans toward larger-than-average pikes. Still, there are enough examples at the small end of the range to show what can be done in as little as 15 square squares, which corresponds to running HO standard gauge 2-8-2s comfortably in a 7 x 12-foot room.

The things we want. Now, before seeing what will fit into various spaces, let's consider what we want in the first place. Not all the things usually considered desirable will appeal to every individual — a swimming pool in the backyard is nice if you like swimming, especially on a hot day, but it may be a minus if you're interested in a minimum-maintenance house and couldn't care less about personal immersion.

However, there are some track plan characteristics that are generally considered more desirable than their alternatives. Using the house analogy again, we can say that all other things being equal, one-story houses are preferred over those that make you go up and down stairs frequently — even by "normal" people who aren't simply looking for the biggest basement per buck for the purpose of accommodating a you know what. It's simply a matter of the relative ease of moving yourself horizontally instead of having to overcome

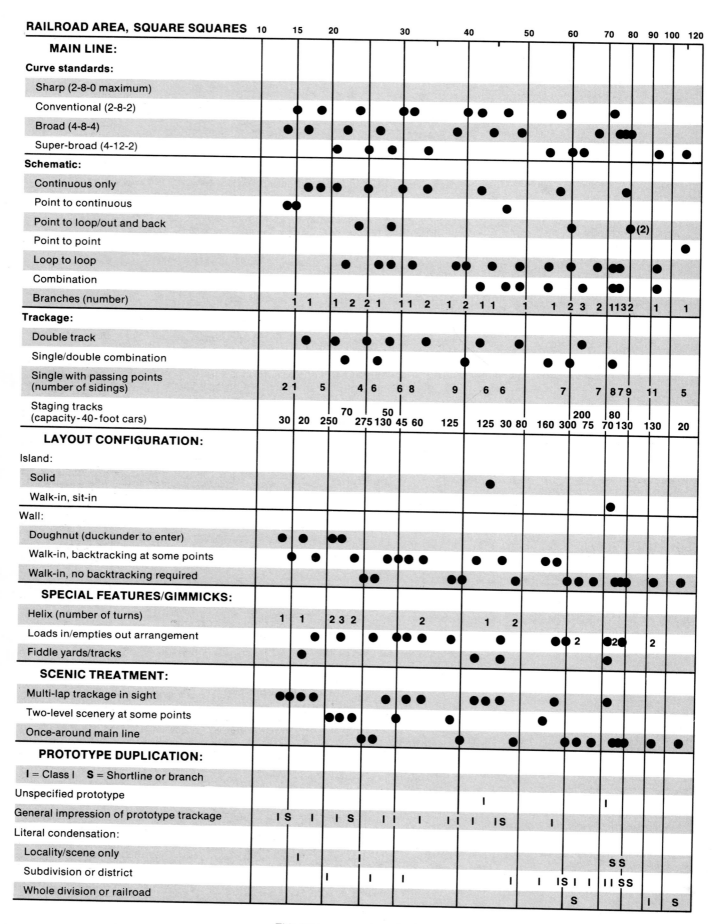

Fig. 2-1 WHAT CAN YOU EXPECT IN YOUR SPACE?

This table summarizes the features of 30 custom-designed track plans, including the 18 in this book. The unit of measure is the "square square," and each layout is represented by a vertical column of dots and data entries.

gravity. In model railroad design there are several such features:

● **Walk-in design.** A railroad civil engineer once said that the first rule for good, easy-to-maintain track is good drainage, that the second rule is more drainage, and that the third rule is still more drainage. In model railroading, we might say that the first rule for an enjoyable layout is good access, the second better access, and so on. This is not only a matter of ease and comfort in building and maintaining the pike; being able to watch the trains run from close up should be a major design goal as well, Fig. 2-4.

So, since we humans have preferred moving around in an erect position for a good many milleniums, a track plan that lets you walk up to most of the points of interest is preferred.

● **And no-backtracking aisleways.** A further refinement of the walk-in pike is one where you can accompany a train over its entire run without hav-

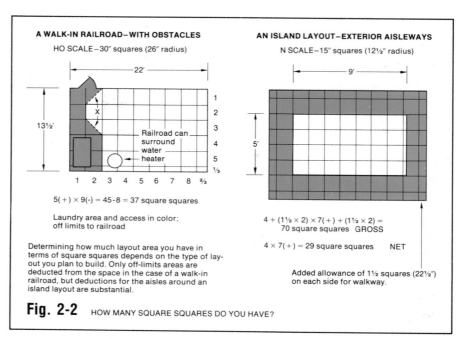

A WALK-IN RAILROAD—WITH OBSTACLES

HO SCALE—30" squares (26" radius)

AN ISLAND LAYOUT—EXTERIOR AISLEWAYS

N SCALE—15" squares (12½" radius)

5(+) × 9(−) = 45-8 = 37 square squares

Laundry area and access in color; off limits to railroad

Determining how much layout area you have in terms of square squares depends on the type of layout you plan to build. Only off-limits areas are deducted from the space in the case of a walk-in railroad, but deductions for the aisles around an island layout are substantial.

4 + (1½ × 2) × 7(+) + (1½ × 2) = 70 square squares GROSS

4 × 7(+) = 29 square squares NET

Added allowance of 1½ squares (22½") on each side for walkway.

Fig. 2-2 HOW MANY SQUARE SQUARES DO YOU HAVE?

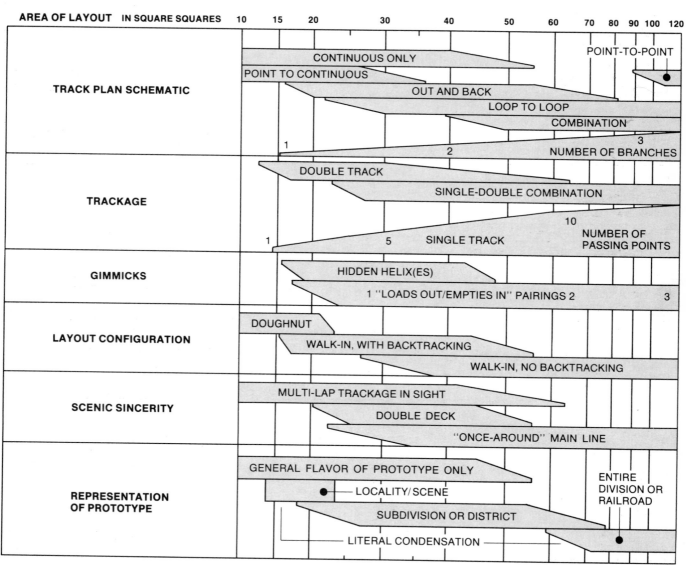

Fig. 2-3 WHERE THINGS ENTER THE PICTURE

Each desirable feature of a "dream layout" requires a certain minimum space. This chart, based on 30 custom-designed railroads, shows the points at which certain features become possible as space available for the layout increases.

Fig. 2-4. A walk-in aisle configuration where an engineer can follow the train over its entire route is by far the most convenient — and realistic — arrangement for a model railroad. This impressive scene showing such a configuration is on the HO layout of the Rensselaer Model Railroad Society in Troy, New York.

MODEL RAILROADER: Andy Sperandeo

ing to backtrack around a peninsula of benchwork or make a duckunder. Now that walk-around controls are available, the logic of such a railroad's main line is much more apparent, and operators achieve a satisfying sense of really being the engineer of a train that is going somewhere for a purpose.

While being a tower operator can be just as much fun as being an engineer — you get to watch lots of trains go by — the pike with walk-around possibilities is still to be preferred. You can operate a walk-around pike comfortably with operators remaining at their wayside positions, but running a non-walk-around layout by yourself (which is the way the vast majority of model railroads are operated most of the time, if questionnaire answers are to be believed) is not at all satisfactory.

So, the first choice for a layout configuration is the no-backtracking walk-in; next comes the walk-in where (usually because some twisting or overlapping is necessary to fit all the lobes of track into the space) all parts of the main line are accessible, but not in station order.

What's the third choice? Usually, it's a pike where a single duckunder gives access to a central operating area from which all points not on the exterior can be comfortably seen and reached. We can, with some stretching, call this the "doughnut" configuration — it may be bent and the hole elongated and twisted, but it's still basically a doughnut since there's only one hole. Way down on the list is the "Swiss cheese" or "gopher prairie" configuration, where access and operation require repeated ducking under to pop up in several foxholes in an essentially solid railroad.

● **A main line that goes somewhere.** Since even the shortest real railroad goes from someplace to someplace else, a model railroad will be more convincing if the "main line" is long enough and arranged so the trains seem to do just that. Whether this means devising a plan that goes from one terminal to another or one that actually has a return loop at one or both ends is more a matter of the desired proportion of switching to running out on the line. Usually, a loop-to-loop schematic is the preferred arrangement, except for large pikes where the main line is so long that you're ready to tie up and turn the train when you finally reach the far end.

Either way, attaining a reasonably long run means folding and wrapping the main line so a lot of it fits within a relatively small area without being too obvious about turning back upon itself. This in turn means making use of view blocks — terrain, trees, buildings, double-faced backdrops, or what have you — to conceal the fact that our trains are actually wandering around in a confined area instead of striking off toward the horizon.

There are two degrees of desirability here. Nicest is the once-around main line where a train goes from one end to the other without using the same track more than once and where only one segment of main line is visible at any point. When the limited has gone by westbound it's *gone*, and you won't see it until it comes back on the return trip; for all you can tell, it may have gone all the way to Chicago or Jacksonville or wherever the imaginary terminal of our railroad is.

Next best is a multi-lap main, where

a lot of the spaghetti is concealed but a complete trip involves passing through the same scenes more than once. If overall operation (particularly, working many trains past each other over a single-track route) is of higher priority than providing realistic scenes to serve as backgrounds for such individual operations as the meeting of two trains, extra mainline length is worth more than the sincerity of only going through each scene once. A twice-around pike packs almost twice the mainline run into the same area, so the choice is more a matter of preference than of right versus wrong.

If much of your traffic is open-top cars where it's painfully evident that you're hauling the same coal back and forth over a point-to-point line (unless you are so sincere as to load and unload the cars on every trip), a schematic which allows continuous running of such consists in one direction may be preferable. A schematic that lets you have it both ways — designated as a "combination" plan in Fig. 2-3 — may be highly desirable.

● **Staging tracks.** We almost always have too much rolling stock to fit on the visible parts of our railroad, and we almost always want to simulate heavier traffic over the main line than can be accounted for by the industries and passenger stations actually represented in the room. The answer in both cases is to provide extensive layover or staging tracks — through (preferably) or stub tracks out of sight but so connected to the visible lines as to conveniently originate or swallow up whole trains, Fig. 2-5.

Less desirable (but still far better than the alternative of grabbing cars out of the main yard when their time on the shelf has come) is the "fiddle yard," usually regarded as a concept of British origin, where this unseemly process is carried out offstage on a set of hidden stub tracks. This fits in almost anywhere and is a scheme worth keeping in mind!

● **Mostly open trackage.** One goal of the basic schematic and aisleway arrangement should be to minimize the amount of non-staging trackage that has to be concealed. Other things being equal, a pike with most of its track visible is to be preferred — you had to pay for it and lay the track, so it's a shame to have to cover it up!

By definition, staging tracks should be hidden from view, but they must also remain readily accessible. These criteria are not necessarily incompatible if cleverness is used in locating staging tracks so they can be approached from above, from below, or from the side. In other situations overall realism can be improved by hiding some of the main line. Where it's necessary to parallel two unrelated segments of the route, the "once around"

effect can be preserved by hiding one of them. Oftentimes a tunnel is the logical way to get by a furnace or under another portion of the railroad.

However, we build more tunnels on model railroads in a week than prototype railroads have accumulated in a century, so we really ought to take it easy with the number of portals we use if we are to be reasonably realistic. In detailing the plan, inconspicuous ways of fading from sight can be used instead of tunnels — curving away behind a hill or failing to emerge after passing beneath an overpass, for example. These improvements often take extra room, though, proving once again that realism becomes easier to achieve the more space you have.

• **A copy of the prototype.** Nothing can look as much like the Pennsy as a four-track Horseshoe Curve or an electrified "flying junction" with the GG1s and m.u. commuter trains zapping over and under each other at speed. The same considerations apply to copying other prototype railroads (though perhaps not at quite the same emotional pitch that the PRR seems to inspire in its fans). Given a reasonable layout area it's simply not possible to fit in literal copies of the trackage and structures of even lesser stations, yards, or mainline segments, but by selectively compressing a carefully chosen chunk of railroad it's often possible to capture the essence of the prototype to the extent that a knowledgeable visitor will agree "Yep, that *is* the Santa Fe," or East Broad Top or Western Maryland.

How big does a layout have to be to represent a specific prototype? As Fig. 2-3 indicates, the answer is more a matter of matching the portion of the line you try to depict to the area available. With smaller pikes only the general impression of a prototype is possible, much of which must come from the rolling stock in evidence. However, if you stick with a single locale or scene (and choose something rural instead of Altoona or Proviso), the flavor can come through even in a 5 x 9-foot pike.

On the other hand, if you are interested in railroading in general but eclectic in your preferences, liking SP Twelve-Wheelers, B & M commuter Moguls, and high-wheeled Lake Shore Prairie types ardently and equally, a free-lance railroad will suit you better than one faithfully patterned after one subdivision of any of those lines. Likewise, if you're modeling a shortline railroad which does well to justify running two trains a day, you have little incentive to squeeze in ten passing tracks between the terminals even though there may be room. On such a pike a 250-car staging yard isn't the best place to spend a chunk of your turnout money, either.

So, how does it come out? Now we have a framework on which to hang the

MODEL RAILROADER: Jim Kelly

Fig. 2-5. The six staging loops on the bottom level of Jim Kelly's N scale layout will eventually be concealed by scenery. Each can hold one or more trains to help generate heavy traffic over the visible portions of the railroad, including the famed Southern Pacific Tehachapi Loop to be located above the staging tracks.

possibilities of any given space. In the broadest terms, if you have a big enough space you can incorporate all the "good" design features we've discussed and include a literal condensation of a fair chunk of whatever prototype railroad territory you want to model — but you don't have to if you don't want to!

Overlapping the sizes somewhat because the distinctions aren't absolute, we can consider what is reasonable to expect in small, medium, and large layout areas:

• **Small pikes — up to 20-22 square squares.** Contrary to what you might expect, some of these modest layouts use super-broad curves because running huge steam locomotives is a top priority.

Schematics are either continuously-only affairs — a simple or twice-around oval or perhaps a folded dogbone — or point-to-continuous schemes, usually operated in out-and-back fashion. There simply isn't room for point-to-point or loop-to-loop arrangements.

Main lines are either double track or single track with less than four passing points unless extremely short trains are to be run. There often is a branch or two, maybe even of a different gauge; these don't take much room.

It must be that the number and length of staging tracks is determined far more by the rolling stock situation than by the space available — staging track capacity in our examples varies from 0 to 250 cars! Clearly, if the job of the railroad is to accommodate a collec-

MODEL RAILROADER: Jim Hediger

Fig. 2-6. This four-layer hidden helix moves trains between the otherwise separate upper and lower levels of Jim Hediger's HO Ohio Southern.

Fig. 2-7. A completed two-level scenic treatment on Dale Stanford's HO Dover Hill Western Railroad. It looks confusing, but while running trains each operator tends to concentrate on his own train, virtually ignoring action on the other level.

MODEL RAILROADER: Jim Hediger

tor's treasure trove and show off a sampling of it, this can be done with little regard to how modest the space may be!

Most railroads smaller than 20-22 square squares are "doughnuts," requiring a duckunder to enter the operating and viewing area. Some are walk-ins, but backtracking is necessary to follow a train over its run — in these limited areas it just isn't possible to work in a long main line without having it loop over itself.

Likewise, trains must make multiple trips past the same point in achieving a modest length of run. If the area is at the upper end of the "small" range — 20 square squares or more — the apparent spaciousness of the railroad can be increased by having two separately scenicked levels at some points, a nice improvement. A two-level pike in a small area, however, requires a gimmick: the hidden helix — perhaps with as many as three complete turns, Fig. 2-6. You can have a small, scenically outstanding railroad, but you have to be prepared to work for it!

Finally, while it's possible to create a general impression of the character of a prototype railroad, it's hard to do much in the way of literally condensing trackage and surroundings in more than a single scene.

● **Medium-size pikes — from 24-25 to 55-60 square squares.** In areas of from 24 to 60 square squares it is almost always possible to have a main

line that goes somewhere. Most are loop-to-loop affairs, often with a continuous-run option. If the main line allows for running continuously in one direction only, this is because that is the desired schematic and not because that is all that will fit. There is room for a single track main if desired, with six or more passing points to make operation interesting and varied.

Staging trackage is again optional, but typically capable of holding 30 to more than 200 cars. A branch or two is typical.

All pikes of this size can be of walk-in configuration; in the case of the larger ones, it's usually possible to follow a train over its whole run without backtracking.

Some pikes provide a satisfactorily long run without passing through the same scene twice; others double back because the extra mileage is worth more than the sacrificed realism. A double-deck scenic treatment to get the best of both worlds may be possible without using a helix if mountain grades are part of the recipe, Fig. 2-7.

Medium-size layouts can begin to achieve a literal condensation of a subdivision of Class I railroad, though most choose to give a general impression of the trackage and scenic surroundings of the railroad as a whole.

● **Large pikes — 60 square squares and up.** Here the walk-in railroad with a loop-to-loop main line (and perhaps

with a continuous-run option) is almost standard. It's also possible to manage a fair representation of two different railroads operating in the same area. If heavy-traffic single-track railroading is desired, there is room for seven to ten — or more — passing points.

It's unlikely that backtracking will be required to follow the main line via the aisleways, and except for the most mileage-hungry, a once-around line which never passes the same scene twice is long enough, and this can be achieved without double-decking. There is no need for a helix or other gimmicks to gain altitude quickly — in fact, the problem may be to keep the railroad from scraping the ceiling at the summit of a long grade!

Pikes this big can reproduce specific features of the prototype (suitably compressed, of course), representing either a major subdivision or district of a Class I route or perhaps an entire short line.

A few common features. You might think that very large pikes always feature super-broad curves, but it's not necessarily so. If locomotives of the very longest and stiffest types are to be absent from the scene, even a railroader with space to burn may opt for broad, rather than super-broad, curves. Medium-size and even small layouts are almost as likely to be designed on the basis of liberal radii to accommodate long cars and big engines with reasonably good appearance.

Branch lines, usually with sharper curves that can be nestled within the mainline loops, are popular in all layout sizes. The "loads in/empties out" gimmick for surreptitiously exchanging open-top cars and maintaining the illusion of real mineral traffic (described in detail in TRACK PLANNING FOR REALISTIC OPERATION) fits well throughout the spectrum of pike sizes, and in the biggest there may be more than one such connection so that more than one commodity may be moved realistically.

Obviously, if a gimmick such as double-decking works to get more railroading into a limited space on a medium-sized pike, the same gimmick can also be used in a large track plan to make it, in effect, still bigger. Is this good? For someone who will have help to build the railroad, who has more than the average amount of time to devote to model railroading, or who is just plain more gung ho than most of us, probably yes. Otherwise, a more relaxed track plan is more appropriate when the space available is in the 75 square square range and above.

But now it's time to return from the land of delightful possibilities to the province of painful reality. In Chapter 3 we'll discuss how the track plan is actually derived from the planning materials package.

Devising the plan

A sequence designed to preclude catastrophic errors

ONCE THE PRIORITIES are in order and some of the likely possibilities based on the size and shape of the area are apparent, the time has come to go to work on the plan itself.

The process of planning on paper is discussed, with examples, in my earlier book, TRACK PLANNING FOR REALISTIC OPERATION. Frankly, although the procedures in Chapters 8, 9, and 10 of that book date from 1963, I don't have anything really new to say about the matter! Track is still just as wide as it was then, obstacles are just as immovable, and except for the advent of high-cube boxcars and tri-level auto racks (assuming you're staying up to date along with your prototype) that require increased vertical clearances, nothing much has changed.

One aspect of custom track planning affects how the plan is drawn. The design has to be presented so that someone else — the customer — can understand and use it. The main effect of this, at least upon me, is that I am more conservative than I otherwise might be when it comes to things that are altogether practical to build but hard to draw!

For example, although there is no reason why two layers of track cannot be exactly over one another, shifting one slightly does make the drawing a lot clearer. In one custom plan I avoided adding a fourth level of track in a stacked-loop area even though the approach grades and alignments were reasonable. It just *looked* (on the plan) as though this would be a hopeless mess! Fortunately in this case the layout builder was sufficiently experienced to recognize that the fourth layer would improve the overall plan — and decided to add it himself. (If that fourth level does prove to be a witch to build, he will only have himself to blame for the stiff neck or skinned knuckles, but I'm sure that the resulting layout will be the better for it.)

In drawing the plan it's doubly important that I avoid serious mistakes which would affect the operability of the pike and which could be difficult or impossible to fix if discovered later. One precaution I've mentioned before is to develop the plan on tracing paper directly over the owner's scaled plan of his space and its obstacles — "Measure twice, cut once!" Other precautions relate to the sequence in which certain steps in completing the design are carried out. For me, doing things in a particular order has turned out to be both time-saving and effective in catching goofs early on. These, in order, are the most helpful procedures:

● **Trust the squares.** I'm relieved to report that the "by the squares" process for sorting out the possibilities of a given area does indeed work, to the extent that I actually use it myself!

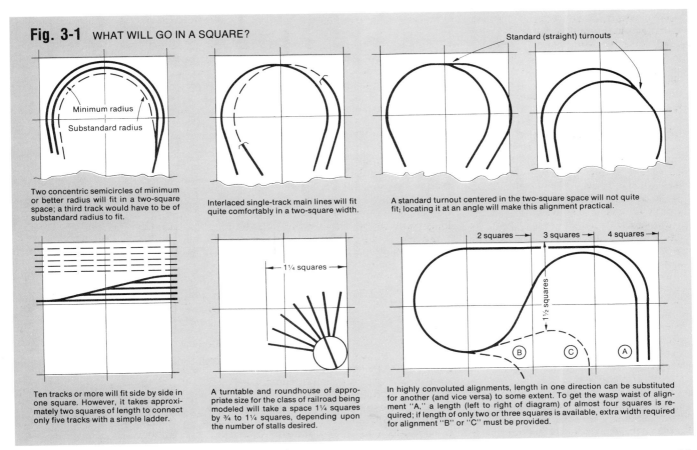

Fig. 3-1 WHAT WILL GO IN A SQUARE?

Two concentric semicircles of minimum or better radius will fit in a two-square space; a third track would have to be of substandard radius to fit.

Interlaced single-track main lines will fit quite comfortably in a two-square width.

Standard (straight) turnouts

A standard turnout centered in the two-square space will not quite fit; locating it at an angle will make this alignment practical.

Ten tracks or more will fit side by side in one square. However, it takes approximately two squares of length to connect only five tracks with a simple ladder.

A turntable and roundhouse of appropriate size for the class of railroad being modeled will take a space 1¼ squares by ¾ to 1¼ squares, depending upon the number of stalls desired.

In highly convoluted alignments, length in one direction can be substituted for another (and vice versa) to some extent. To get the wasp waist of alignment "A," a length (left to right of diagram) of almost four squares is required; if length of only two or three squares is available, extra width required for alignment "B" or "C" must be provided.

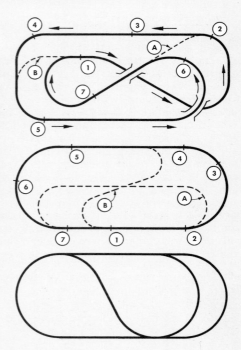

Fig. 3-2 TRACK PLAN SCHEMATICS

The "schematic" of a track plan shows the relative location of tracks and turnouts without regard for their physical position in the layout. Both of the right-hand plans have the schematic at the left.

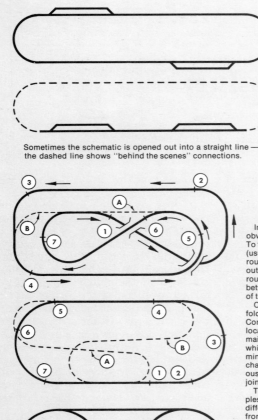

Sometimes the schematic is opened out into a straight line — the dashed line shows "behind the scenes" connections.

In many track plans, the schematic is far from obvious, as in these two look-alikes.

To find the schematic, find one continuous route (usually you should look for the longest possible route a train can take without going over a turnout twice). Mark consecutive points off on this route at convenient intervals (at least one point between each turnout location). Mark direction of travel at all points.

Open this route out into an oval, eliminating folds and twists. Mark off oval in same way. Connecting tracks such as "A" and "B" are then located by observing where they hook up to the main line (with respect to the numbers) and in which direction. It will then be possible to determine whether they are reversing tracks (which change the direction of a train over the continuous route) or merely alternate routes (which rejoin the main line in the same direction).

The schematics can then be sketched in simplest form. We find that the plans are radically different operationally — trains can change only from clockwise to counterclockwise running on the plan at the right. This is a generally unsatisfactory arrangement in a layout of this type.

The locations of cutoff tracks "A" and "B" make all the difference.

KALMBACH BOOKS: A. L. Schmidt

Fig. 3-3. Intended for measuring distances on maps, an opisometer is a handy gadget for track planning. As the wheel at the bottom is rolled along a line, the needle indicates the distance, which you can then convert to the appropriate units for your plan.

There's no need to say more about it, other than to repeat the standard caution that has appeared with various descriptions of the squares concept in books and magazines over the years: *Don't cheat!* If things don't look like they'll fit, they won't, Fig. 3-1. Optimistically squeezing a 180-degree curve into 1¾ squares instead of the required two will catch up with you later; either the size of the square must be reduced — if you have started out with a minimum radius bigger than you must have for your particular equipment and operation — or else a different arrangement must be tried. Neither solution is much of a problem when the plan is at the stage of determining what scheme will fit in terms of squares, since only a little time has been spent in sketching.

On the other hand, whenever the squares have indicated that a scheme should fit, the plan has always worked out in the scale drawing — it has never been necessary to admit defeat and go back to square one!

● **Use a convenient drawing scale.** One inch to the foot seems like a nice, even scale for a finished track plan drawing, but it will drive you up the

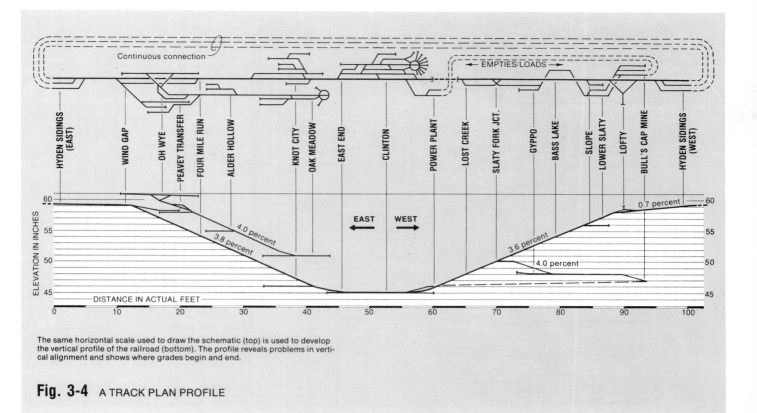

The same horizontal scale used to draw the schematic (top) is used to develop the vertical profile of the railroad (bottom). The profile reveals problems in vertical alignment and shows where grades begin and end.

Fig. 3-4 A TRACK PLAN PROFILE

wall: An inch on the layout is $1/12''$ on the drawing, which is $2/3$ of an eighth or, if you prefer, $1\frac{1}{3}$ sixteenths — see the problem? There are architect's scales capable of handling the matter, of course, but it's easier to use $3/8$, $3/4$, or $1\frac{1}{2}$ inch to the foot scales where $1/32''$, $1/16''$, or $1/8''$ translates to a nice even inch on the pike.

● **Use train height as the unit for preliminary vertical figuring.** Where tracks will have to go over and under one another it's usually sufficient to rough in elevations by figuring that the upper track must be one "unit" above the lower. The unit — about three inches in HO — is the railhead-to-railhead vertical separation required to get one track over the other. It takes a few squares to get up there without impossible grades, but closely figuring actual percentages can wait until later. The important thing to remember early on is that tracks must cross either at grade or at least one whole unit apart (except in flip-over wind-up train toys!).

● **Make a schematic.** Eventually the the drawing progresses to where the main line fits, passing tracks have been fitted in, and the yard is located and connected. After a few refinements — tracks shifted to get rid of bad S-curves, to put the main line through the straight side of turnouts wherever possible, and to make the trackage look as much like a real railroad as space permits — I make a schematic of the whole plan.

The schematic, Fig. 3-2, shows, in straightened-out format, how the var-ious lines on the layout interconnect, making it apparent how trains can be run (and how they can't be). The schematic isn't strictly necessary for constructing the railroad, and working things out so that each line is connected up precisely as on the plan can be a head-scratcher. As a check on how the railroad will operate, though, the schematic is more than worth the trouble. More often than not, I find at least one surprise — a crossover that looks logical in the yard plan but turns out to be "backward" so far as letting trains move through as they should, passing track spacings that would create worse-than-intended bottlenecks when traffic gets heavy, or even connections missing completely.

● **Measure the trackage.** As part of drawing the schematic to scale (in the horizontal, or along-the-line, direction only), it's necessary to measure the main line fairly accurately. Just waving a ruler around the curves isn't good enough. An opisometer (the neat map measuring gadget that consists of a dial indicator geared to a wheel that you roll along the line, Fig. 3-3) is quick and accurate (albeit usually calibrated in units that take a calculator to straighten out), but hardly worthwhile if you're only planning one layout. A piece of soft wire bent around the curves and straightened out for measurement on a scale will do just as well, and the reasonable accuracy it provides is worth the trouble.

● **Make a profile.** Next, using the same horizontal scale as on the sche-matic, I work out a profile of the main tracks, including all yards and branches, Fig. 3-4. The profile shows the ups and downs of the railroad, revealing the steepness and length of grades and helping to clarify the vertical clearance situation. Where tracks cross over each other the minimum separation required is known, and if electrical service cabinet doors, gas meters, or other obstacles determine how high or low a portion of the line must be, these segments serve as vertical benchmarks that must be observed and accommodated.

Now precise grades can be determined, and at this point it's highly probable that some major adjustments will have to be made — including, perhaps, changes in horizontal alignment. To reduce and balance grades I may have to shift considerably the locations where tracks cross each other, but it's a lot easier now than later — when the layout owner would have to do it with a saw instead of an eraser. Only now are elevations put on the track plan.

● **Look at some cross sections.** Where horizontal and vertical alignments get really messy, working out cross sections may be helpful. Is that line on the lower level as inaccessible as it looks on the plan, or can it be reached from below or from the rear to cope with an emergency? The cross section, Fig. 3-5, will tell.

Cross sections can be equally important in suggesting feasible scenic treatments, particularly if an eye-level "horizon" line is included so you can tell in advance what will and will not be visi-

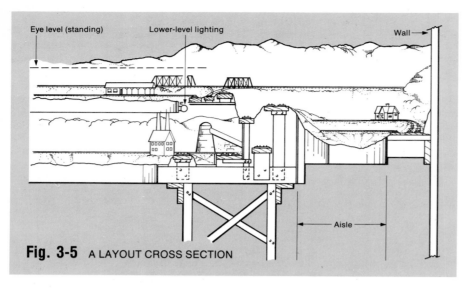

Fig. 3-5 A LAYOUT CROSS SECTION

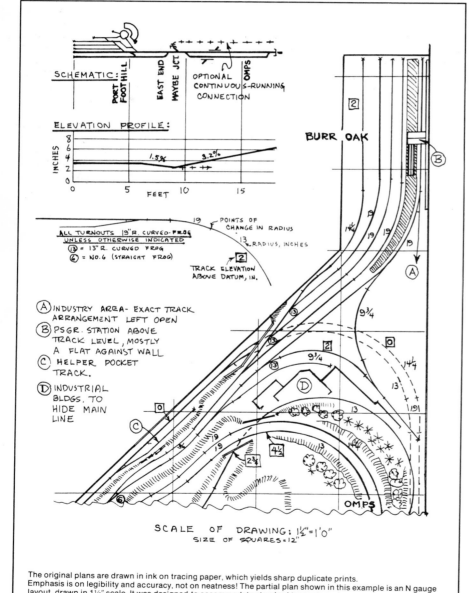

The original plans are drawn in ink on tracing paper, which yields sharp duplicate prints.
Emphasis is on legibility and accuracy, not on neatness! The partial plan shown in this example is an N gauge layout, drawn in 1½" scale. It was designed to accommodate standard turnouts and curves. This reproduction is not to scale.

Fig. 3-6 AN EXAMPLE OF A FINISHED CUSTOM PLAN

ble in the completed scene. At this stage it is still worthwhile to shift trackage to make the railroad more impressive scenically, easier to build and operate, or both.

What does the customer get? When the roar of the electric eraser has died away and the last swatch of scrap tracing paper has been consigned to the wastebasket, I'm ready to mail the model railroader who commissioned the plan a package that describes his unique model railroad. Typically, the package includes the basic track plan, a top-level plan if the layout is layered to the point of confusion, a schematic, a profile, critical cross sections, and a tape cassette with about 45 minutes of what I call "disc jockey chatter." This rambling and verbose commentary describes the degree to which some of the customer's objectives had to be modified, unexpected goodies that I was able to work in, and how the finished plan relates to what he said he wanted, explaining specifically why the tracks, aisles, and scenic features are the way they are and how trains can be expected to operate.

My emphasis in drawing, as evident from Fig. 3-6, is definitely not on neatness or finish! Ahead of either of those niceties comes accuracy, to the degree necessary to ensure things will fit and allow the layout builder to launch into construction with confidence.

During actual construction larger-scale working sketches will be prepared, section by section, by the layout builder as required to plan the benchwork. For the larger pikes, much of the translation from drawing to full scale can take place directly on site via chalk marks on the floor. While it wasn't planned that way, if you have 12" floor tiles in your train room the grids on most of the drawings will be directly applicable.

About the plans in this book. In selecting the 18 examples that follow, the editor and I have chosen (in as non-autocratic a fashion as you could hope for, unbiased by the fact that in our hearts we both know exactly what is best for everybody) the custom plans we think will be of most interest and direct help to the most model railroaders. As is the case with any published track plan, benefits which may rub off onto your model railroading will depend on your own inventiveness in seeing things in these examples — ideas, principles, segments, perhaps even a whole schematic — that you can adapt to your own needs and desires.

Each plan includes a "givens and druthers" chart based on the owner's questionnaire and available-space diagram. The brief narrative description accompanying each plan is confined mostly to what's particularly different about the layout as a result of the requirements and desires it seeks to satisfy. Since you have your own givens and druthers, the fact that the sketchy discussion here leaves many of the possibilities and limitations of each plan for you to discover for yourself shouldn't be too much of a loss.

Interpreting the drawings. Curvature is usually not marked on the drawings for those bends of minimum radius which typically account for much of the main line. Likewise, to reduce clutter the radius of parallel curved tracks is not called out on the drawings.

Easements — curves of gradually increasing radius inserted between the straight track and the circular portion of curves, also called "spirals," or "transition curves" — have been universally requested by those ordering plans so far, which speaks well for the judgment of those using custom planning. However, easements are not specifically shown on the drawings of layouts using curves wider than conventional standards because, given the scale of the drawing, the deviation from a circular curve is not much more than the width of the line. In practice, what this means is that the nominal curve radius is reduced by the amount of the offset (as discussed on page 73 of the second edition of TRACK PLANNING FOR REALISTIC OPERATION) and easements are worked in as the track is being laid. The slight reduction in radius will not affect reliability; far more important is maintaining a uniform, kink-free radius throughout the curve.

Easements are shown on a few extremely tight plans with small-radius curves. Such plans are drawn to a larger scale and the point of transition from easement to circular curve is indicated by a double tick mark.

Elevations are to the railhead and are shown as colored, boldface figures, usually indicating height in inches above nominal floor level. Floors, particularly in basements, aren't always level, so the builder must keep this in mind and adjust the layout if the plan is to work as designed. In cases where the area is such that the whole railroad can be higher or lower without running afoul of windows, pipes, or whatever, the elevations are with reference to some datum — usually zero at the lowest point on the main line.

The profiles are on a standardized grid so that interpreting their significance will become easier as you keep looking at and comparing them.

To make the distinction between track lines and the edges of the benchwork perfectly clear the edges of the benchwork are usually shown as being a series of straight lines. While it's not too likely the track and the edges of the layout would be confused in a simple plan, when you get to plans with multiple layers or wild aisleway arrangements it is easier to visualize quickly what's going on if the track is curved but the layout edge is "bent." However, in building layouts nowadays we generally round off the corners, and that's

really what is intended in many areas on these plans.

Turnouts are keyed on the individual plans. Most owners have indicated that some or all turnouts were going to be handbuilt, but a sizable minority indicate a desire to use ready-made turnouts or commercially available turnout kits. Non-availability in the most widely used lines of commercial trackwork (Lambert and Atlas) of the turnout size that best matches up with the curves used on most layouts (the No. 5) is unfortunate. Because of this, in many of the track plans No. 6 turnouts have been used wherever their additional length doesn't seriously compromise the design.

On a happier note, curved turnouts (either rigid or adjustable-radius) are increasingly available, and a high proportion of those shown in these plans fit the geometry of commercially available units, whether or not the layout builder plans to hand-lay his own.

Finally, the cornball station names shown on many of the drawings are non-binding, especially on the owner of the layout. There is a space on the questionnaire for the owner to supply his own station designations, but if he doesn't I have to identify key points somehow, and the puns can get pretty bad! If you should be so blessed as to have one of these plans coincide with your space and givens and druthers, by all means feel free to rename the towns any way you want!

The Kentucky Cumberland Railroad

A loop-to-loop main line with an important branch, both tailored to passenger operation

Southern Railway

The locale for the Kentucky Cumberland will be the hill country of Kentucky and Indiana, and the KC scene along the Little Ohio River may well look a lot like this stretch of the Southern Railway between Oakdale and Chattanooga, Tennessee.

THE KENTUCKY CUMBERLAND is a railroad set in the present day, and its proprietor has elected to depict the autumn season, when its locale — the wooded hill country of Kentucky and Indiana — is a riot of colorful foliage. "The railroad runs a highly profitable passenger service over its entire length, frequently aiding Amtrak on routes in the Southeast," he states; "I am otherwise in touch with reality." Well, full-length passenger cars in long consists *are* attractive, and being able to build a railroad that has them in the 1980s demonstrates one of the truly fine aspects of model railroading: the ability to rise above prototypical financial considerations!

The space available for the layout is 14' x 20' 6". Designing an HO gauge passenger-service-oriented railroad for such a modest space demands a careful balancing act involving minimum radius, reasonable aisle widths, and the number of tracks that can be included at tight spots; otherwise, operating possibilities might be unduly subordinated to accommodating those long cars. By using easements and curved turn-

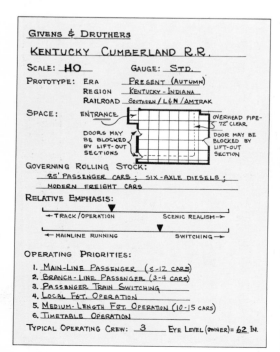

GIVENS & DRUTHERS

KENTUCKY CUMBERLAND R.R.

SCALE: **HO**   GAUGE: **STD.**

PROTOTYPE: ERA   PRESENT (AUTUMN)
            REGION   KENTUCKY - INDIANA
            RAILROAD   SOUTHERN / L&N / AMTRAK

SPACE: ENTRANCE   OVERHEAD PIPE-
                                           72" CLEAR
           DOORS MAY   DOOR MAY BE
           BE BLOCKED   BLOCKED BY
           BY LIFT-OUT   LIFT-OUT
           SECTIONS   SECTION

GOVERNING ROLLING STOCK:
    85' PASSENGER CARS ; SIX-AXLE DIESELS ;
    MODERN FREIGHT CARS

RELATIVE EMPHASIS:

    ⊢————————▼——————————————————⊣
      ←TRACK/OPERATION   SCENIC REALISM→

    ⊢————————————————▼————————⊣
      ←MAINLINE RUNNING   SWITCHING→

OPERATING PRIORITIES:

    1. MAIN-LINE PASSENGER (8-12 CARS)
    2. BRANCH-LINE PASSENGER (3-4 CARS)
    3. PASSENGER TRAIN SWITCHING
    4. LOCAL FGT. OPERATION
    5. MEDIUM-LENGTH FGT. OPERATION (10-15 CARS)
    6. TIMETABLE OPERATION

TYPICAL OPERATING CREW: __3__   EYE LEVEL (OWNER) = __62__ IN.

Charles B. Castner

The Kentucky Cumberland is sufficiently compact that there won't be room to model Louisville's Union Station, shown here in 1971, but the layout's variety of routings means that the free-lance station that there is space for will see far more trains than does the prototype.

18

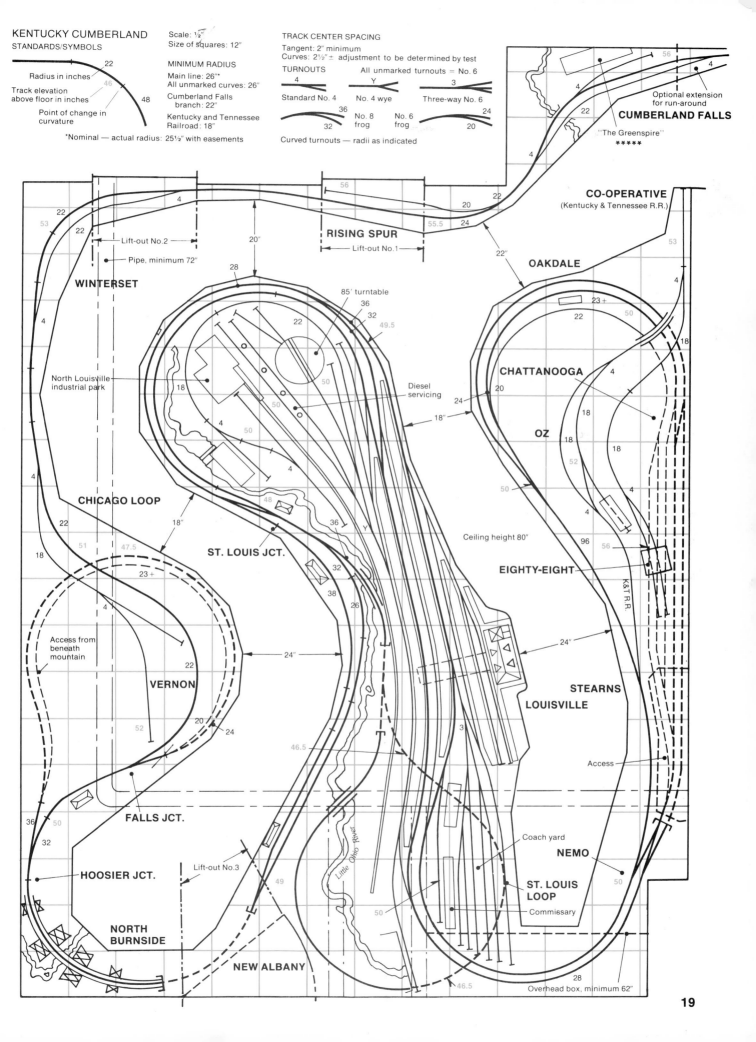

KENTUCKY CUMBERLAND
STANDARDS/SYMBOLS

Radius in inches — 22
46
48

Track elevation above floor in inches

Point of change in curvature

*Nominal — actual radius 25½" with easements

Scale: ½"
Size of squares: 12"

MINIMUM RADIUS
Main line: 26"*
All unmarked curves: 26"
Cumberland Falls branch: 22"
Kentucky and Tennessee Railroad: 18"

TRACK CENTER SPACING
Tangent: 2" minimum
Curves: 2½"± adjustment to be determined by test

TURNOUTS   All unmarked turnouts = No. 6

4
Standard No. 4

Y
No. 4 wye

3
Three-way No. 6

36
32
No. 8 frog

No. 6 frog

24
20

Curved turnouts — radii as indicated

CUMBERLAND FALLS
56
4
Optional extension for run-around
4
22
"The Greenspire"
*****

CO-OPERATIVE
(Kentucky & Tennessee R.R.)

56
22
20
22
55.5
24
53
4

RISING SPUR
Lift-out No.1

Lift-out No.2

20"

Pipe, minimum 72"

WINTERSET
22
53
22
22
4

4

28

85' turntable
36
32
49.5

22

50

18

50

50

4
50
4

48

OAKDALE
23 +
22
50
4

CHATTANOOGA
20
18
OZ
18
52
18
4
50
4
96
56

18"
Diesel servicing
24

North Louisville industrial park

CHICAGO LOOP
18"
22
51
47.5
18
23 +
4

36
Y

36
32
38
26

ST. LOUIS JCT.

Access from beneath mountain

VERNON
22
52
20
24

Ceiling height 80"

EIGHTY-EIGHT

K&T R.R.

24"
STEARNS
LOUISVILLE

Access

FALLS JCT.

46.5
24"

3

HOOSIER JCT.
36
50
32

Lift-out No.3
49

NORTH BURNSIDE

NEW ALBANY

Little Ohio River

50

Coach yard

NEMO

ST. LOUIS LOOP
Commissary
50

28
Overhead box, minimum 62"
46.5

19

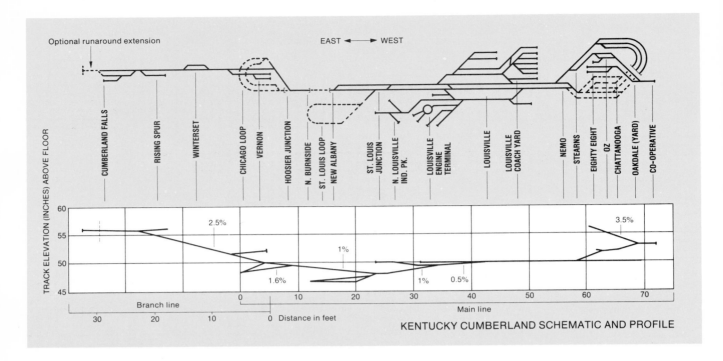

Optional runaround extension

EAST ← → WEST

CUMBERLAND FALLS
RISING SPUR
WINTERSET
CHICAGO LOOP
VERNON
HOOSIER JUNCTION
N. BURNSIDE
ST. LOUIS LOOP
NEW ALBANY
ST. LOUIS JUNCTION
N. LOUISVILLE IND. PK.
LOUISVILLE ENGINE TERMINAL
LOUISVILLE
LOUISVILLE COACH YARD
NEMO
STEARNS
EIGHTY EIGHT
OZ
CHATTANOOGA
OAKDALE (YARD)
CO-OPERATIVE

TRACK ELEVATION (INCHES) ABOVE FLOOR

60

55   2.5%   3.5%

50   1%

45   1.6%   1%   0.5%

0   10   20   30   40   50   60   70

Branch line   Main line

30   20   10   0   Distance in feet

KENTUCKY CUMBERLAND SCHEMATIC AND PROFILE

outs (of the proportions now commercially available), it is possible to achieve reliable operation and good appearance with a nominal minimum mainline radius of 26″, which in this case results in an area approximately 5½ x 7 squares.

To suit the proprietor's top priorities — passenger-train switching and operation of respectably long through limiteds — the schematic emphasizes variety of routing rather than attempting to provide a long mainline run by making multiple passes through the same scenes. Aisle width is squeezed to 18″ at two points, but both bottlenecks are short and lead to wider spots where members of the small operating crew can decompress.

By making full use of the rugged plateau terrain appropriate for the locale and the aid of a section of double-faced backdrop separating Louisville and St. Louis Junction it's possible to keep the Chattanooga, Chicago, and St. Louis return loops and far-side trackage out of sight with only five tunnels. Also, this is "Rat Hole Division" territory, so the result, even with a considerable number of tunnel portals, will be scenically sincere.

In keeping with the Southern and L & N prototype lines in Kentucky mainline grades are moderate — sufficient to allow tracks to overlap each other comfortably, but no more. Short, fairly steep pitches coming up out of the river valleys are sufficient to test the mettle of high-speed passenger power hauling long consists, but all the longer grades are moderate; this railroad is definitely not helper country.

Making the most of the along-the-wall space. Even without the extra consideration of providing limited (liftout section) access to the three door-

ways in the layout area, it's difficult to make good use of all the along-the-wall space in any situation where entry to the railroad is from the side, as it is here. A branch line does this best, since it can depart the main line without having to come back and can wiggle along on a narrow shelf without taking too much space away from the rest of the railroad.

The Kentucky Cumberland has a fairly long branch running up to a five-star hotel so grand as to rate its own connecting train (Pullman car equipped, no less!) from the nearest terminal. This branch to Cumberland Falls features somewhat sharper curvature than the main line (22″, which could be widened to mainline standards without much problem if the long cars insist) and a lot steeper grades, primarily in the interest of making clear that it is a branch. If sneaking a track through the entrance doorway far enough for locomotives to make a run-around move at the Falls terminal isn't politically possible, some genuine ingenuity will be required to figure out the most efficient way to run the branch.

What about non-passenger trains? Subordinating the demands of motive power and the needs of freight trains to the expanse of station and coach yard trackage needed to achieve the feel of a major passenger terminal is required in this plan, but the relative compactness of modern diesel facilities comes to the rescue at Louisville. The Kentucky Cumberland keeps a Pacific and a Ten-Wheeler on the roster for fan trips, so the turntable and pair of stall tracks left in place when the rest of the steam facilities were torn out are worthwhile.

The possibilities for local freight operation are good. A tall building at the

North Louisville industrial park anchors the crowded mill and plant scene and its switchback spurs, and is also a logical terminus for the freestanding backdrop.

Kentucky has always been full of busy short-line connections such as the Kentucky & Tennessee, which joins the Kentucky Cumberland at Stearns. Fitting easily above the essential return loop and staging tracks serving the main line, its track is steep, crooked, and switchbacked. Traffic coming off the K & T will be taken to Louisville by the Kentucky Cumberland local freight and will often have to roost on a passenger track while awaiting pickup by a through freight train, but there's nothing wrong with that if schedules are coordinated properly — an essential aspect of any passenger pike.

The compromises. As is likely to be the case in ambitious mainline-oriented pikes as compact as this one, there is only a general correlation between station names and sequences on the model and the corresponding prototype geography. Among other transgressions, I have been most disrespectful to the mighty Ohio River in heading for Indiana en route to Chicago and St. Louis. Likewise, there is no attempt to represent either of Louisville's passenger stations or their operating and track arrangements.

Work up a realistic schedule of originating, through, and terminating trains for and from points east, north, and south, all of them with interconnecting through sleepers and head-end cars, though, and when you are in the thick of all the switching there will be no doubt at all that the big passenger yard in the middle of the Kentucky Cumberland Railroad truly *is* Louisville.

The Ash Fork & Maricopa Railroad and the Apache Tram Railroad

A double-deck, point-to-loop main line shoehorned into an attic — with roll-around access!

PER CUBIC FOOT occupied, the Ash Fork & Maricopa has to be one of the most efficient plans in the business. Its 8' x 14' attic site would not be unduly confining were it not for the sloping ceiling which descends to only 34" above the floor where it intersects the rear wall. Given the ceiling's 8:12 slope, the last 5' of room width is below stand-up height, so a walk-in plan is out of the question.

Furthermore, the minimum mainline radius which can comfortably accommodate HO standard gauge 4-6-4s and full-length heavyweight passenger cars (the difference between their 80-foot length and five-foot-longer stream-

liners is fairly significant when you're forced to cut things close) is 22"; appearance won't be the greatest, but for short consists it's a curve we can live with. Put three circles of this mainline radius in the available space and it quickly becomes clear that an aisleway snaking among them will be barely 18" wide. Although this is basically a one-person railroad, that 18" is still awfully narrow.

A swivel chair to the rescue. The solution offered here is a roll-in track plan, an arrangement in which most of the operation and moving around within the layout is done seated in a swivel chair. This allows (with care in design

to minimize the depth of the under-track benchwork structure and keep it all well above knee level) the main line to start out at 34" above floor level and still be both comfortable to operate and effective in appearance.

Since heads (even including ears) are considerably narrower than shoulders, the skinny 18" aisle becomes OK because its boundaries are above seated neck height. The mainline track between Ash Fork and Prescott which must cross over the entrance to the railroad at a low 53" elevation also becomes a fairly comfortable roll-under for our seated railroader.

There is stand-up ceiling height (72")

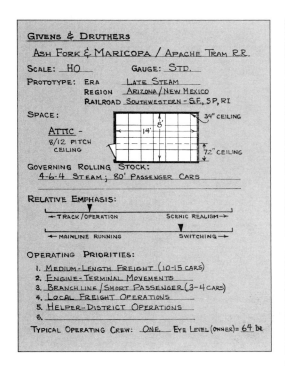

GIVENS & DRUTHERS

ASH FORK & MARICOPA / APACHE TRAM R.R.

SCALE: HO   GAUGE: STD.

PROTOTYPE: ERA   LATE STEAM
           REGION   ARIZONA/NEW MEXICO
           RAILROAD   SOUTHWESTERN - S.F, SP, RI

SPACE:

ATTIC -
8/12 PITCH
CEILING

GOVERNING ROLLING STOCK:
4-6-4 STEAM; 80' PASSENGER CARS

RELATIVE EMPHASIS:

← TRACK/OPERATION   SCENIC REALISM →

← MAINLINE RUNNING   SWITCHING →

OPERATING PRIORITIES:
1. MEDIUM-LENGTH FREIGHT (10-15 CARS)
2. ENGINE-TERMINAL MOVEMENTS
3. BRANCHLINE/SHORT PASSENGER (3-4 CARS)
4. LOCAL FREIGHT OPERATIONS
5. HELPER-DISTRICT OPERATIONS
6.

TYPICAL OPERATING CREW: ONE   EYE LEVEL (OWNER) = 64 IN.

Equipment on the Ash Fork & Maricopa will be a study in contrasts. Mainline power for the big hill between Prescott and Woods Junction is likely to include chunky 2-8-2s like Santa Fe 3232 (top right). Branchline operations will call for lighter locomotives, perhaps along the lines of this Southern Pacific 2-8-0 (right) shown on the Espee Cloudcroft Branch in New Mexico in 1946.

Richard H. Jahns

Charles M. Mizell Jr.

along the front of the railroad, so by locating the top-level trackage in this area, a two-level layout becomes possible. When the train moves topside from its low originating point the change of viewpoint is easy — you just stand up!

And a pair of helixes. Almost since the time of Archimedes the solution to connecting radically different track elevations via a main line of practical steepness (albeit difficult — but pusher operations are well up on the priorities list here) has been available in the form of the helix. Using two of them in this case and ascending at a steady 4 percent, the Ash Fork & Maricopa gains almost 20″ between Helper and the summit at Ash Fork. The big hill is about one scale mile long — not bad for so compact a railroad when you consider that some notable prototype grades such as New York Central's West Albany Hill weren't any lengthier.

Down-and-back operation from Ash Fork, the only real yard for which we can eke out room, to an end-of-the-line loop with a substandard-radius (20″) layover siding is the best we can do in the space. Breaking up, turning, and remaking trains at the stub terminal is going to be challenging, but the fact that mainline running over that awesome helper district isn't going to set any speed records means that a fair balance between terminal and over-the-road operations will be achieved.

Seven percent on the tram! Although the helixes eat up a good deal of the available real estate, there are still some nooks and crannies at low and middle elevations to provide a suitable stamping ground for a tiny logging Shay and a short but scenically distinct branch, the Apache Tram. The switchback branch, which features a minimum radius of 16″ and includes a stretch of 7 percent grade, departs the main line at Woods Junction and runs to Mill Valley, No. 1 Switchback (where the tail track is located on the door!),

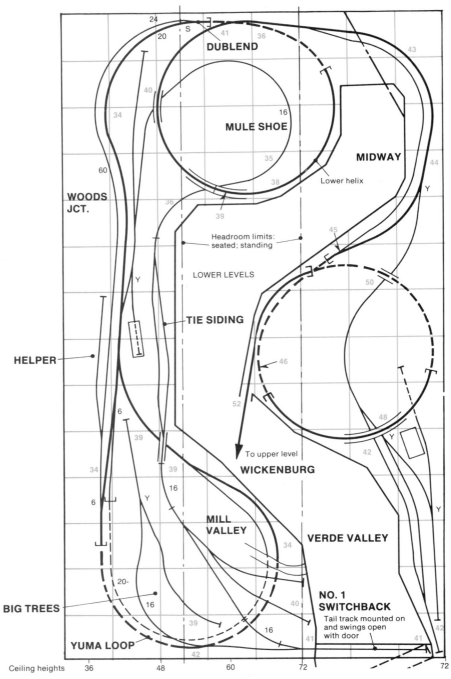

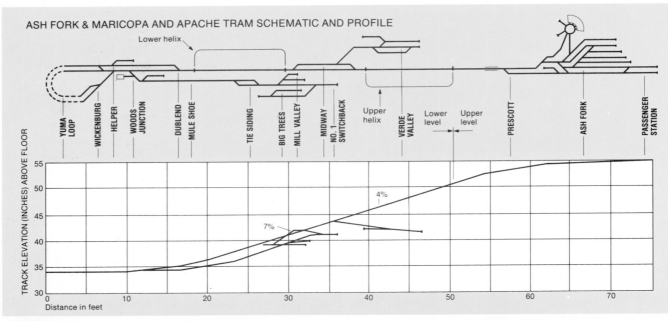

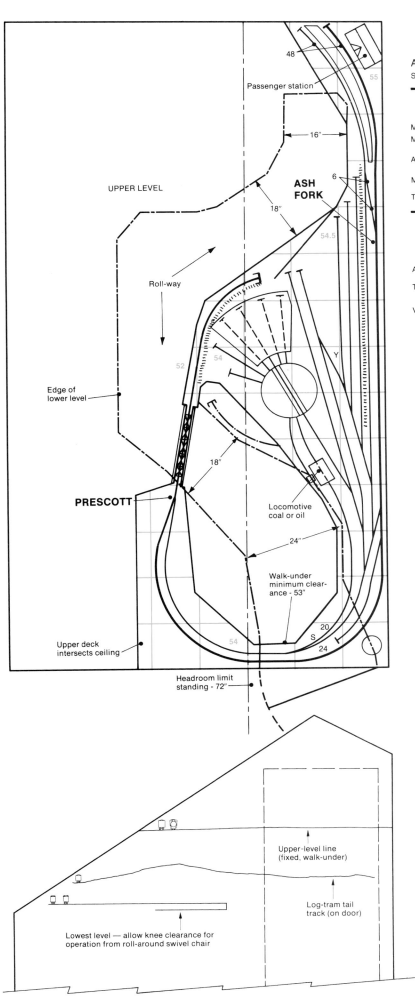

UPPER LEVEL

Passenger station

48

55

16"

ASH FORK

6

18"

Roll-way

54.5

Edge of
lower level

52   54

Y

18"

PRESCOTT

Locomotive
coal or oil

24"

Walk-under
minimum clear-
ance - 53"

Upper deck
intersects ceiling

20
S   24
54

Headroom limit
standing - 72"

Upper-level line
(fixed, walk-under)

Log-tram tail
track (on door)

Lowest level — allow knee clearance for
operation from roll-around swivel chair

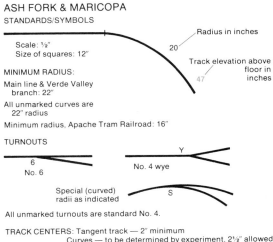

ASH FORK & MARICOPA
STANDARDS/SYMBOLS

Radius in inches

20

Track elevation above
floor in inches

47

Scale: ½"
Size of squares: 12"

MINIMUM RADIUS:
Main line & Verde Valley
branch: 22"
All unmarked curves are
22" radius
Minimum radius, Apache Tram Railroad: 16"

TURNOUTS

6   Y

No. 6   No. 4 wye

Special (curved)   S
radii as indicated

All unmarked turnouts are standard No. 4.

TRACK CENTERS: Tangent track — 2" minimum
Curves — to be determined by experiment, 2½" allowed

VERTICAL SEPARATION: Railhead-to-railhead:
3" minimum (22 scale feet)

and Big Trees. The Apache Tram's main function is to enhance the local freight fun for peddler runs working their way up and down the big hill. Another short branch to Verde Valley even has room for a short run-around track at the end so it can be operated as much more than a mere spur, thereby providing considerable interest for local freights calling at Midway.

Construction of a layout as crowded as this one must be reasonably precise — there simply isn't much margin for error in getting all those tracks over and under each other at the numerous crossing points. But, as is always the case with one of these little giants, overall there isn't a great deal of construction to be done, and the railroad is highly practical as a one-man affair.

Scenery as you go. Given that track locations are pretty well determined by the three-dimensional confinement, how can we arrive at the most effective scenic treatment? Designing as you build is likely to be the best procedure here, because trying to predict where to locate trees so they give a good impression of a forest when some of them must intersect and be cut off by that sloping ceiling is far from easy. The best approach is to wait and see how things look as the hardshell or screen wire goes into place.

What about operating those medium-length 10- to 15-car trains on such a compact railroad, the owner's top-priority item? The key is in the use of sections of what could almost be considered double track at each end of the line. Fairly long (by model railroad standards) trains can be doubled together on these tracks, then sent out. Adroit dispatching will be required to ensure that these long trains won't have to meet anything beyond saw-by length at Midway's short siding.

The Northwest Pacific Railroad

This double-deck HO layout features big engines and a variety of traffic patterns

IF BIG MOTIVE POWER is what you like, it can be worth whatever it takes to give it a place to run — smaller engines just can't do the same things for you as those big articulateds or turbines or DD40s. The HO gauge Northwest Pacific is a prime example of putting first things first under what would seem to be most trying and unpromising circumstances.

The 12' x 16' 6" basement room available for the layout has no "give" to it, with four unyielding walls. Furthermore, in order to avoid a permanently built-in railroad in the face of a high probability of future moves, the proprietor has specified that two of the walls are to be left free for displays, with aisles adjacent from which to view them — at least it is assumed that young eyeballs or strong glasses will allow viewing from the 24"-wide aisle.

The essential motive power includes huge, 2-8-8-4 Yellowstones of the long-cabbed Duluth, Missabe & Iron Range variety, high-wheeled Northern Pacific 4-8-4s for passenger service, and those enormous eight-axle, two-engine diesel units. Thirty inches is the minimum mainline radius, bringing the usable space to a little over three by four squares. Obviously, this design is going to have to work the third dimension for all it's worth, and fortunately the top priority is depicting helper district operations, with some way of running mainline-length passenger trains a close second.

Long trains in restricted space. The most fundamental way of achieving long-train capability in restricted space is with some form of dogbone. In the loop-to-loop arrangement on the Northwest Pacific there is a short section of single track midway in the bone's shank to slow things down a bit and make the typical trip from the lower-end knob to the upper turnaround take a little longer. At a reasonable 3.5 percent grade it's possible to reach an upper level almost 20" above the lower loop — ample height for the two-deck scenic treatment and enough room for comfortable tracklaying down below even after the upper level is in place.

En route between the levels there are some close clearances as the main track winds its way upward, and access to the main operating area within the hole of this two-layer doughnut has to be via a duckunder. But, there is a 45'-long helper district, and that's more than long enough to put the whole train on the grade and clearly demonstrate why making a run for the hill won't help. Forty-five feet of 3.5 per-

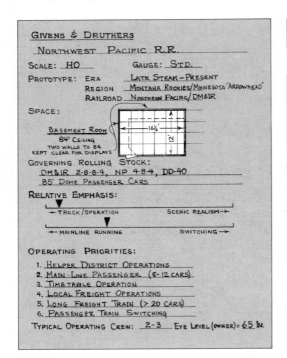

GIVENS & DRUTHERS

NORTHWEST PACIFIC R.R.

SCALE: HO   GAUGE: STD.

PROTOTYPE: ERA   LATE STEAM - PRESENT
REGION   MONTANA ROCKIES/MINNESOTA "ARROWHEAD"
RAILROAD   NORTHERN PACIFIC/DM&IR

SPACE:

BASEMENT ROOM — 16½'
84" CEILING
TWO WALLS TO BE
KEPT CLEAR FOR DISPLAYS — 12'

GOVERNING ROLLING STOCK:
DM&IR 2-8-8-4, NP 4-8-4, DD-40
85' DOME PASSENGER CARS

RELATIVE EMPHASIS:

← TRACK/OPERATION   SCENIC REALISM →

← MAINLINE RUNNING   SWITCHING →

OPERATING PRIORITIES:
1. HELPER DISTRICT OPERATIONS
2. MAIN-LINE PASSENGER (8-12 CARS)
3. TIMETABLE OPERATION
4. LOCAL FREIGHT OPERATIONS
5. LONG FREIGHT TRAIN (> 20 CARS)
6. PASSENGER TRAIN SWITCHING

TYPICAL OPERATING CREW: 2-3   EYE LEVEL (OWNER) = 65 IN.

According to its owner, the setting for the HO gauge Northwest Pacific will combine elements of the Northern Pacific's spectacular crossing of the Rocky Mountains in Montana (top right) and the Duluth, Missabe & Iron Range's Arrowhead country in Minnesota (right). Incidentally, the DM & IR 2-8-8-2 in the photo will be one of the smaller locomotives on this railroad!

Northern Pacific

Franklin A. King

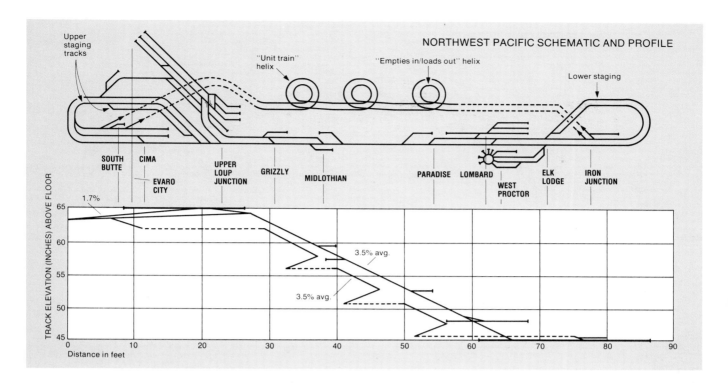

cent is a very respectable helper grade in HO scale — the only drawback is that the rest of the main line has to be represented by staging loops at each end!

Simulating mineral traffic. Mineral traffic (iron ore in this case) is the backbone of the Northwest Pacific's business, so we need an empties-in/loads-out arrangement connecting the mine and smelter ends of the railroad or else a continuous-run arrangement that lets the loaded trains move repeatedly in one direction, while the empties do the opposite. With the aid of that friend of all really cramped track plans, the helix (here it takes a three-turn one), we can have both. In fact, the varied train, car, and engine routings possible on this little giant of a layout fill up a sizable diagram!

I've indicated two places on the upper level plan where liberties might be taken with the aisleway specifications to add precious inches to both ends of the Evaro City passenger facilities. Every inch of every track is absolutely crucial in assembling trains and getting them headed into their appropriate routes with necessary motive power attached in the right places fore and aft, but it can be done. There are a few tracks here and there that will keep the local freight busy too, but the crew had better have things well organized before setting out on its run.

Also critical to good operation is the exact alignment of crossovers with respect to those short straightaways if S-curve problems are to be kept within limits. Only the fact that 24' ore cars will handle the bulk of the traffic permits reliable uncoupling-ramp locations for some of the key movements in

simulating the huge flow of loads of the heavy rust from mine to mill and vice versa. There will have to be some research and development in ways to handle trains and cars safely on this

railroad, too — if a string of loads gets away from you at the top of the helix they may come sailing out the bottom end at Iron Junction with truly devastating realism!

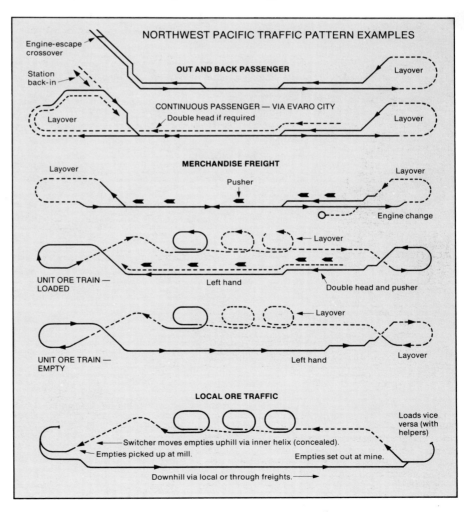

25

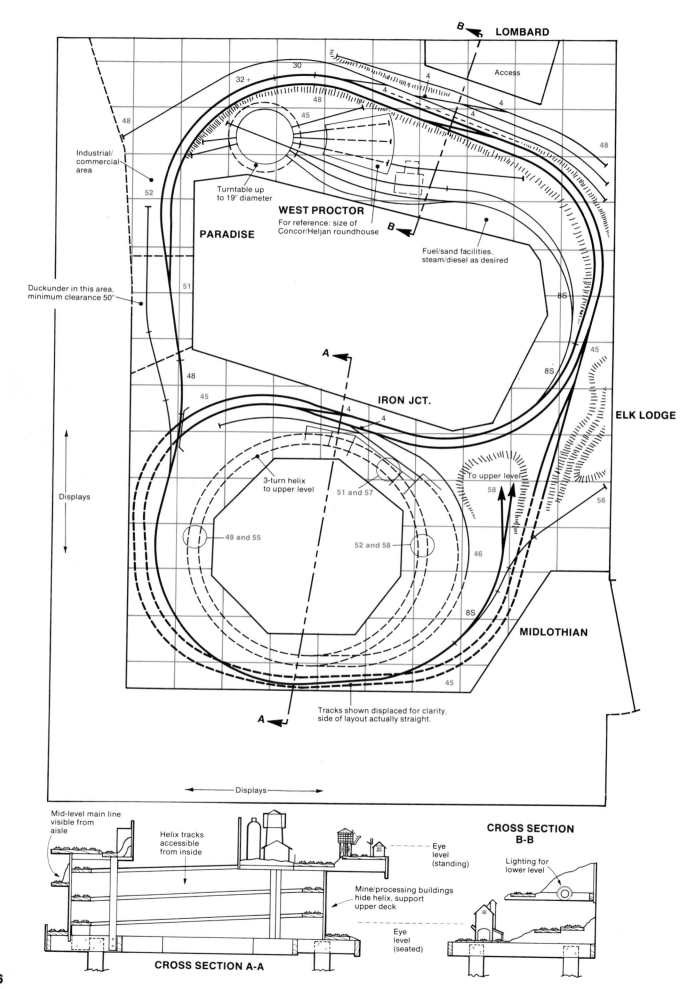

LOMBARD

Access

30

32 +

48

45

4
4
4
4

48

48

52

Industrial/
commercial
area

Turntable up
to 19" diameter

WEST PROCTOR

For reference: size of
Concor/Heljan roundhouse

PARADISE

B

Fuel/sand facilities,
steam/diesel as desired

Duckunder in this area,
minimum clearance 50"

51

8S

8S

45

48

45

A

IRON JCT.

4

4

ELK LODGE

Displays

3-turn helix
to upper level

51 and 57

To upper level

58

56

49 and 55

52 and 58

46

8S

MIDLOTHIAN

45

A

Tracks shown displaced for clarity,
side of layout actually straight.

Displays

Mid-level main line
visible from
aisle

Helix tracks
accessible
from inside

CROSS SECTION
B-B

Eye
level
(standing)

Lighting for
lower level

Mine/processing buildings
hide helix, support
upper deck

Eye
level
(seated)

CROSS SECTION A-A

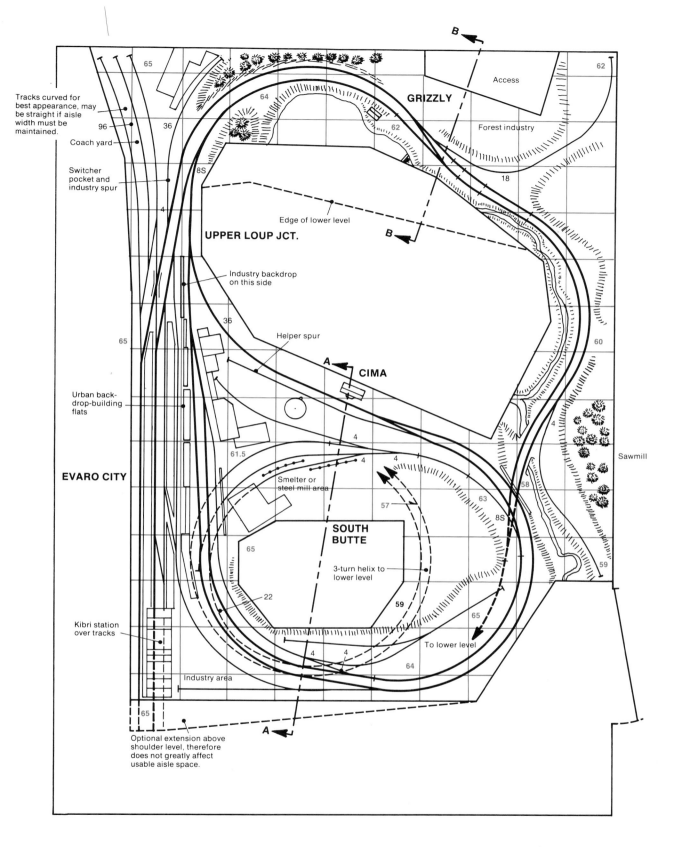

Tracks curved for best appearance, may be straight if aisle width must be maintained.

65

96

36

Coach yard

8S

Switcher pocket and industry spur

4

64

62

GRIZZLY

Access

Forest industry

18

62

B

Edge of lower level

UPPER LOUP JCT.

B

Industry backdrop on this side

36

Helper spur

A

CIMA

65

Urban back-drop-building flats

60

Sawmill

EVARO CITY

61.5

4

4

4

Smelter or steel mill area

57

63

8S

58

SOUTH BUTTE

65

3-turn helix to lower level

59

59

22

65

Kibri station over tracks

To lower level

64

4

4

Industry area

65

A

Optional extension above shoulder level, therefore does not greatly affect usable aisle space.

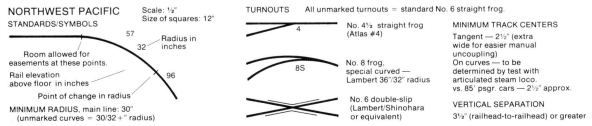

NORTHWEST PACIFIC
STANDARDS/SYMBOLS

Scale: ½"
Size of squares: 12"

57
Radius in inches
32

Room allowed for easements at these points.

Rail elevation above floor in inches

Point of change in radius

96

MINIMUM RADIUS, main line: 30"
(unmarked curves = 30/32 +" radius)

TURNOUTS   All unmarked turnouts = standard No. 6 straight frog.

4
No. 4½ straight frog (Atlas #4)

8S
No. 8 frog, special curved — Lambert 36"/32" radius

No. 6 double-slip (Lambert/Shinohara or equivalent)

MINIMUM TRACK CENTERS

Tangent — 2½" (extra wide for easier manual uncoupling)
On curves — to be determined by test with articulated steam loco. vs. 85' psgr. cars — 2½" approx.

VERTICAL SEPARATION

3½" (railhead-to-railhead) or greater

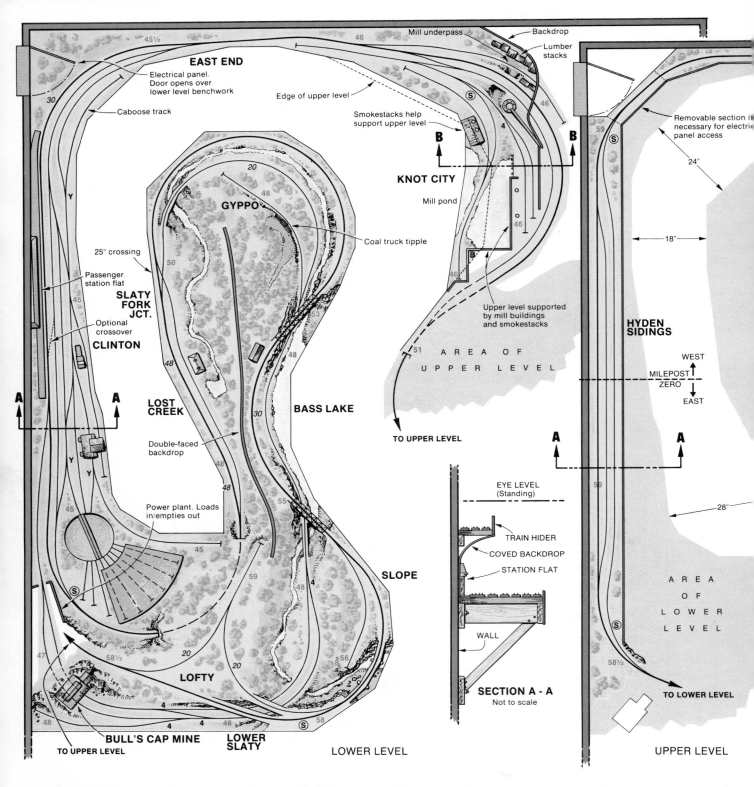

EAST END
Electrical panel.
Door opens over
lower level benchwork

Caboose track

Mill underpass

Backdrop
Lumber
stacks

Edge of upper level

Smokestacks help
support upper level

KNOT CITY

Mill pond

Removable section if
necessary for electric
panel access

24"

HYDEN
SIDINGS

18"

WEST

MILEPOST
ZERO

EAST

GYPPO

Coal truck tipple

25° crossing

Passenger
station flat

SLATY
FORK
JCT.

Optional
crossover

CLINTON

Upper level supported
by mill buildings
and smokestacks

AREA OF
UPPER LEVEL

LOST
CREEK

Double-faced
backdrop

BASS LAKE

SLOPE

TO UPPER LEVEL

AREA
OF
LOWER
LEVEL

Power plant. Loads
in/empties out

EYE LEVEL
(Standing)

TRAIN HIDER
COVED BACKDROP
STATION FLAT

WALL

SECTION A - A
Not to scale

LOFTY

BULL'S CAP MINE

LOWER
SLATY

TO UPPER LEVEL

LOWER LEVEL

TO LOWER LEVEL

UPPER LEVEL

The Appalachian Southern Railroad

An HO double-deck mainline railroad with an HOn3
logging branch on the upper level — all in 14' x 15'

THE APPALACHIAN SOUTHERN
is a standard gauge road handling substantial long-distance freight traffic
through (and over) the mountains of
Tennessee. It's in a mining and timber

area where narrow gauge lumbering
has survived into the late steam era.
Passenger train evolution has stopped
short of streamliners, but both local
and through trains traverse the rug-

ged, beautiful scenery two or three
times a day. Like neighbors Southern
and L & N, the Appalachian Southern
defers to its curvature by relying on
relatively modest-sized motive power

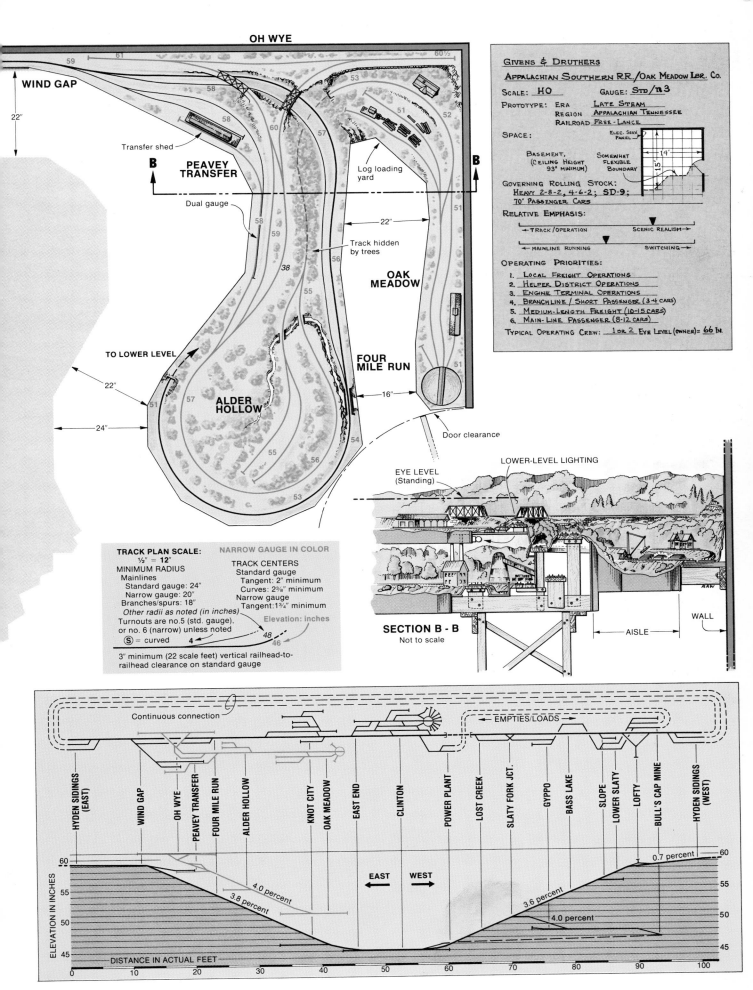

OH WYE

WIND GAP

22"

Transfer shed

B
PEAVEY
TRANSFER

Dual gauge

Log loading
yard

Track hidden
by trees

OAK
MEADOW

B

22"

38

FOUR
MILE RUN

TO LOWER LEVEL

22"

24"

ALDER
HOLLOW

16"

Door clearance

59 61 60½ 53 51 52 51 51 51

58 60 57 56 54 55 56 53 c.

58 59 55 57 55 51

GIVENS & DRUTHERS

Appalachian Southern R.R./Oak Meadow Lbr. Co.

SCALE: HO   GAUGE: STD/n3

PROTOTYPE: ERA   LATE STEAM
           REGION APPALACHIAN TENNESSEE
           RAILROAD FREE-LANCE

SPACE: ELEC. SERV.
                                PANEL
        BASEMENT,   SOMEWHAT   14'
        (CEILING HEIGHT FLEXIBLE
        93" MINIMUM)   BOUNDARY   15'

GOVERNING ROLLING STOCK:
    HEAVY 2-8-2, 4-6-2; SD-9;
    70' PASSENGER CARS

RELATIVE EMPHASIS:
    ← TRACK/OPERATION   SCENIC REALISM →
    ← MAINLINE RUNNING   SWITCHING →

OPERATING PRIORITIES:
    1. LOCAL FREIGHT OPERATIONS
    2. HELPER DISTRICT OPERATIONS
    3. ENGINE TERMINAL OPERATIONS
    4. BRANCHLINE / SHORT PASSENGER (3-4 CARS)
    5. MEDIUM-LENGTH FREIGHT (10-15 CARS)
    6. MAIN-LINE PASSENGER (8-12 CARS)
TYPICAL OPERATING CREW: 1 OR 2 EYE LEVEL (OWNER)= 66 IN.

TRACK PLAN SCALE: NARROW GAUGE IN COLOR
    ½" = 12"
MINIMUM RADIUS   TRACK CENTERS
  Mainlines   Standard gauge
    Standard gauge: 24"   Tangent: 2" minimum
    Narrow gauge: 20"   Curves: 2⅜" minimum
  Branches/spurs: 18"   Narrow gauge
    Other radii as noted (in inches) Tangent: 1¾" minimum
  Turnouts are no.5 (std. gauge),   Elevation: inches
  or no. 6 (narrow) unless noted
  (S) = curved   48
                                          4   46
3" minimum (22 scale feet) vertical railhead-to-
railhead clearance on standard gauge

LOWER-LEVEL LIGHTING

EYE LEVEL
(Standing)

SECTION B - B
Not to scale

AISLE   WALL

Continuous connection   ← EMPTIES/LOADS →

HYDEN SIDINGS (EAST) | WIND GAP | OH WYE | PEAVEY TRANSFER | FOUR MILE RUN | ALDER HOLLOW | KNOT CITY | OAK MEADOW | EAST END | CLINTON | POWER PLANT | LOST CREEK | SLATY FORK JCT. | GYPPO | BASS LAKE | SLOPE | LOWER SLATY | LOFTY | BULL'S CAP MINE | HYDEN SIDINGS (WEST)

EAST ← → WEST

ELEVATION IN INCHES

60

60
4.0 percent
3.8 percent   0.7 percent
55   3.6 percent   55
50   4.0 percent   50
45   45

DISTANCE IN ACTUAL FEET
0   10   20   30   40   50   60   70   80   90   100

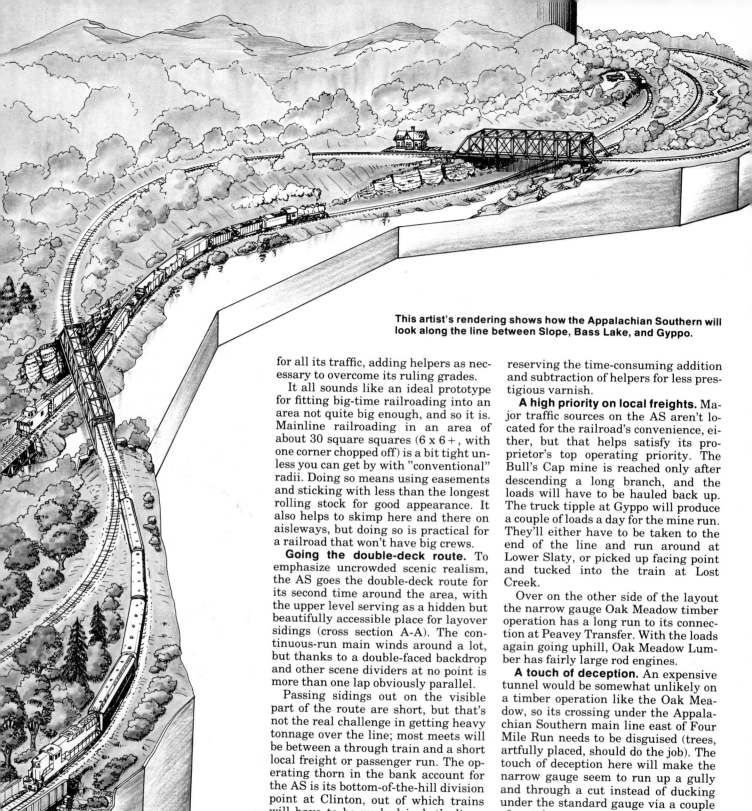

This artist's rendering shows how the Appalachian Southern will look along the line between Slope, Bass Lake, and Gyppo.

for all its traffic, adding helpers as necessary to overcome its ruling grades.

It all sounds like an ideal prototype for fitting big-time railroading into an area not quite big enough, and so it is. Mainline railroading in an area of about 30 square squares (6 x 6+, with one corner chopped off) is a bit tight unless you can get by with "conventional" radii. Doing so means using easements and sticking with less than the longest rolling stock for good appearance. It also helps to skimp here and there on aisleways, but doing so is practical for a railroad that won't have big crews.

Going the double-deck route. To emphasize uncrowded scenic realism, the AS goes the double-deck route for its second time around the area, with the upper level serving as a hidden but beautifully accessible place for layover sidings (cross section A-A). The continuous-run main winds around a lot, but thanks to a double-faced backdrop and other scene dividers at no point is more than one lap obviously parallel.

Passing sidings out on the visible part of the route are short, but that's not the real challenge in getting heavy tonnage over the line; most meets will be between a through train and a short local freight or passenger run. The operating thorn in the bank account for the AS is its bottom-of-the-hill division point at Clinton, out of which trains will have to be pushed in both directions. Westbound helpers can turn on the wye at Lofty after their stints on the 3.6 percent, but those cutting off at Wind Gap will have to drift back down to Clinton tender-first.

Two grades arranged back to back imply that there must be at least two more grades on the railroad to get trains up to the summits from whence they ride the thrilling roller coaster into and out of Clinton, so it's reasonable to run first-line passenger trains double-headed over the entire district,

reserving the time-consuming addition and subtraction of helpers for less prestigious varnish.

A high priority on local freights. Major traffic sources on the AS aren't located for the railroad's convenience, either, but that helps satisfy its proprietor's top operating priority. The Bull's Cap mine is reached only after descending a long branch, and the loads will have to be hauled back up. The truck tipple at Gyppo will produce a couple of loads a day for the mine run. They'll either have to be taken to the end of the line and run around at Lower Slaty, or picked up facing point and tucked into the train at Lost Creek.

Over on the other side of the layout the narrow gauge Oak Meadow timber operation has a long run to its connection at Peavey Transfer. With the loads again going uphill, Oak Meadow Lumber has fairly large rod engines.

A touch of deception. An expensive tunnel would be somewhat unlikely on a timber operation like the Oak Meadow, so its crossing under the Appalachian Southern main line east of Four Mile Run needs to be disguised (trees, artfully placed, should do the job). The touch of deception here will make the narrow gauge seem to run up a gully and through a cut instead of ducking under the standard gauge via a couple of portals.

To the contrary, the Appalachian Southern, being a full-fledged main line in the home country of the "Rat Hole" Division, can properly duck in and out of sight as necessary through rock or masonry portals. To accommodate a cramped situation behind the Knot City mills where an intestinal loop of the narrow gauge must be kept out of sight we can resort to mill buildings and stacks of drying lumber to let the standard gauge main disappear unobtrusively.

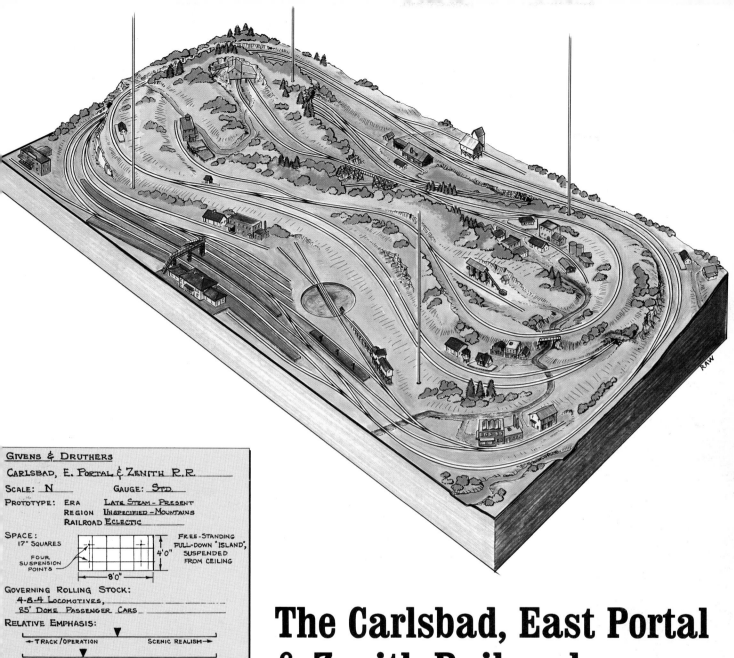

GIVENS & DRUTHERS

CARLSBAD, E. PORTAL & ZENITH R.R.

SCALE: N   GAUGE: STD.

PROTOTYPE: ERA   LATE STEAM - PRESENT
           REGION   UNSPECIFIED - MOUNTAINS
           RAILROAD ECLECTIC

SPACE:
  17" SQUARES   FREE-STANDING
                                 PULL-DOWN "ISLAND",
                          4'0"   SUSPENDED
  FOUR   FROM CEILING
  SUSPENSION
  POINTS
            ← 8'0" →

GOVERNING ROLLING STOCK:
  4-8-4 LOCOMOTIVES,
  85' DOME PASSENGER CARS

RELATIVE EMPHASIS:
         ▼
  ← TRACK / OPERATION   SCENIC REALISM →

         ▼
  ← MAINLINE RUNNING   SWITCHING →

OPERATING PRIORITIES:
  1. MEDIUM-LENGTH FREIGHT (10-15 CARS)
  2. MAIN-LINE PASSENGER (8-10 CARS)
  3. LONG FREIGHT TRAIN OPERATION (>20 CARS)
  4. COMMUTER TRAINS/TRAFFIC
  5. LOCAL FREIGHT OPERATIONS

TYPICAL OPERATING CREW: ONE   EYE LEVEL (OWNER)=N.A. IN.

The Carlsbad, East Portal & Zenith Railroad

A lot of N scale railroading in 4' x 8' —
and designed to hang from the ceiling!

BECAUSE THE CARLSBAD, EAST PORTAL & ZENITH will be required to handle fairly large motive power and long trains in minimum area, in it I've departed from the out-and-back schematic I usually favor for providing a good mix of terminal switching and mainline running in a space equivalent to about three by five squares. Since its proprietor wants it to be a "railroad in suspension" — up against the ceiling between operating and building sessions but accessible from all sides when in the lowered position — it can have a hidden lower level underlying most of its topside area.

At 4' x 8' all areas of the layout are accessible from the edges, while N scale greatly magnifies the "one sheet of plywood" space. Even such massive locomotives as Sante Fe 4-8-4s are expected to (and do!) go around sharp curves in N. A 13" radius (equivalent to a conventional bend of about 24" in HO) is enough to ensure reliable operation in most cases. As it turns out, it's possible to raise the ante to 14½" for at least one track throughout the main line and for most layover tracks. If the CEP & Z should ultimately have some power that is picky about 13" curves, the big engines will still be able to

make it around the railroad with some attention on the part of the dispatcher in planning their routing.

The appearance of the *Limited*'s 85' passenger cars and of long-overhang engines will still suffer somewhat, of course, so more generous curves have been used wherever possible. The worst of the bends will presumably be made less obvious by judicious location of scenic features and structures. A thoroughly prototypical curve extends right through Elm Grove, the one principal passenger station which the layout can afford, and it's right up front where all the good things it does for the train-

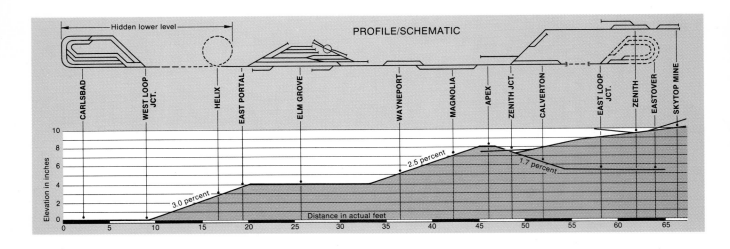

PROFILE/SCHEMATIC

Hidden lower level

CARLSBAD · WEST LOOP JCT. · HELIX · EAST PORTAL · ELM GROVE · WAYNEPORT · MAGNOLIA · APEX · ZENITH JCT. · CALVERTON · EAST LOOP JCT. · ZENITH · EASTOVER · SKYTOP MINE

Elevation in inches

3.0 percent

2.5 percent

1.7 percent

Distance in actual feet

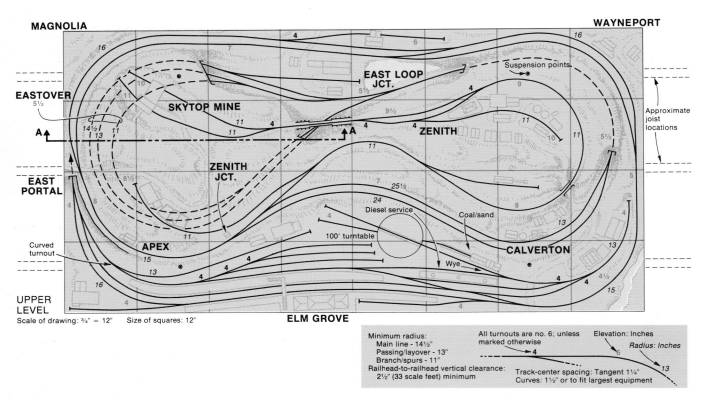

MAGNOLIA

WAYNEPORT

EASTOVER
5½

EAST LOOP JCT.

SKYTOP MINE

Suspension points

Approximate joist locations

A

ZENITH

ZENITH JCT.

EAST PORTAL

Curved turnout

APEX

Diesel service

100' turntable

Wye

Coal/sand

CALVERTON

UPPER LEVEL

Scale of drawing: ¾" = 12"   Size of squares: 12"

ELM GROVE

Minimum radius:
  Main line - 14½"
  Passing/layover - 13"
  Branch/spurs - 11"
Railhead-to-railhead vertical clearance:
  2½" (33 scale feet) minimum

All turnouts are no. 6; unless marked otherwise

Elevation: Inches

Radius: Inches

Track-center spacing: Tangent 1¼"
  Curves: 1½" or to fit largest equipment

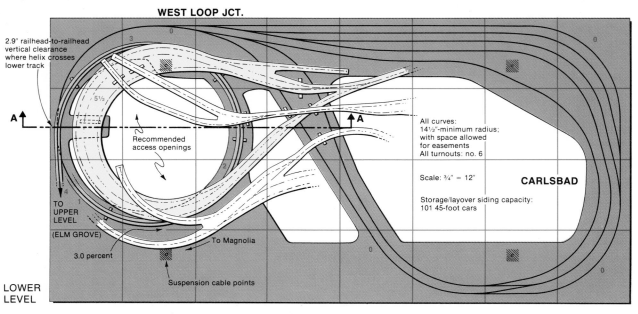

WEST LOOP JCT.

2.9" railhead-to-railhead vertical clearance where helix crosses lower track

A

Recommended access openings

TO UPPER LEVEL
(ELM GROVE)

3.0 percent

To Magnolia

Suspension cable points

All curves:
14½"-minimum radius;
with space allowed
for easements
All turnouts: no. 6

Scale: ¾" = 12"

CARLSBAD

Storage/layover siding capacity:
101 45-foot cars

LOWER LEVEL

32

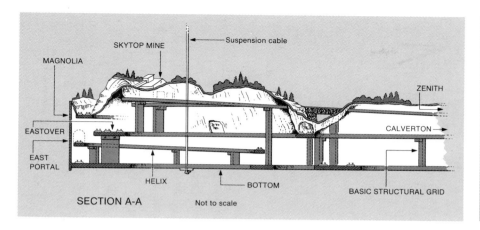

SECTION A-A   Not to scale

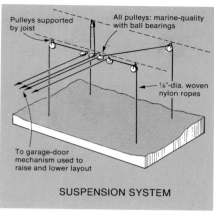

SUSPENSION SYSTEM

watcher are most readily appreciated.

Once again, a helix. Given these concessions it becomes possible to meet requirements for operation and layover of fairly long trains by going to the one practical way of building a two-layer pike in such severely limited space: a helix. This separates the levels by about 4″ — plenty so far as the height of N scale rolling stock is concerned, but just about the absolute minimum finger space required for taking care of the inevitable (though 'tis hoped rare) operational incidents. This plan isn't for a mountain-climbing railroad with helper engines as a big part of the fun, and the 3 percent grades in the helix should be no problem for most N scale trains because traction tires are common and the engine-to-car weight ratio is high.

As cross section A-A shows, access to the helix has to be from below, but that's no problem, since the railroad can simply be hauled up toward the ceiling to make this not only possible but almost comfortable. The lower-level layover trackage is likewise accessible from both an interior hole and from the outside. All turnouts have been carefully kept close to the exterior, even to some extent at the expense of layover-track length. The CEP & Z should nonetheless be able to run at least one freight in the 30- to 40-car

range without completely immobilizing all other traffic on the railroad.

Structural design matters. It goes without saying that the structural design of a railroad like this is not a casual matter. Added to the requirement that the whole business float up into the stratosphere (powered by a garage-door opener mechanism) is a top-to-bottom height restriction of about a foot, to provide sufficient under-the-layout clearance when the room is being used for other purposes.

Essentially, the rigidity needed for a suspended railroad must come from the I-beam effect of the basic structural grid sandwiched between the plywood layers that form the upper and lower track supports. Particularly in N scale, any flexing will be very apparent in terms of the size of the trains.

Building the CEP & Z presumes planning the structure completely before taking saber saw to the virgin 4 x 8 plywood sheets, then working from the bottom up to lay, check out (by operation), and wire the hidden track. The nice part is that on a pike of this scope there isn't all that much to be done before the golden spike can be pushed into place.

Landscape among the joists. Some scenery can rise up into the spaces between the overhead joists, and the Zenith/Skytop trackage has been located

to take advantage of joist locations. As in any small, island-type track plan, it's extremely desirable that the terrain rise high enough along the central spine of the layout to separate the two sides visually, and the extra few inches between the joist locations can ensure success in this respect. If the situation is marginal, rubber trees atop the ridge are always a possibility!

The CEP & Z's builder also included a cosmetic requirement that the underside of the suspended platform be reasonably presentable. This can be met by keeping the access-opening segments cut from the lower-level plywood sheet and arranging them to slide over and hide the gaping wounds.

A practical railroad — in no space. With all this complexity, what's practical in 4′ x 8′? Thanks to the wonders of 1/160 scale, the main line stretches almost two scale miles from loop to loop, there is on-track capacity for hiding 100 cars or so in the "basement" (although this will still be primarily a "sampler" railroad, on which only a selection of the owner's extensive roster will be operating at any given time), and the Magnolia/Wayneport lap sidings allow considerable flexibility in handling long and short trains in a variety of traffic patterns. For a net space requirement (*exclusive occupancy*, that is) of zero, not too bad!

The Maine & Vermont Railroad

New England in HO scale: A continuous double-track main line with a single reversing connection and a switchback quarry branch

THE MAINE & VERMONT Railroad is to be located in the front room of one of those high-ceilinged, immaculate Victorian houses that make small towns in Maine or Vermont look exactly as small towns in Maine or Vermont *should* look. Even though much of the 13' x 19' room must be subordinated to such mundane uses as file cabinets and desks, there is a cheerful area dominated by a deep bay window in which a railroad can find a home if access to those slender double-hung windows can be maintained (for washing, of course). How much the layout may intrude into the office space is a matter of some negotiability, but another window with access requirements similar to those in the bay tends to set a practical limit to the overall size of the railroad.

The Maine & Vermont is well named; it is to be characteristic of northern New England in the late steam/early diesel era, with a touch of poetic license in favor of running a financially disastrous number of short freight, passenger, and even commuter trains on a line that's still neat, prosperous in appearance, and stable despite the modest industrial and population bases in evidence. In its assumed course from southern Maine across New Hampshire and into Vermont the line has no lack of those two wonderful modeling aids to scenic plausibility: mountains and trees. Both are to be used freely and without apology to explain the main line's convolutions and to hide trackage that must be physically adjacent but counties away on the schematic.

Almost two scale miles of main line. And so it develops — a basically double-track, continuous-run main line which combines the 22″ radius appropriate for its motive power with the somewhat narrow aisles satisfactory for a one-person layout to fold almost two scale miles into the area. The aisle configuration is fully walk-in, but much of the operation is on an out-and-back basis from the relatively ample terminal at Winthrop with its two stub passenger tracks to a run-around conclusion at Auburn or to the return loop at Carrabasset. Its elevated and exposed site prevents the return loop from serving as a hidden staging track, but its trestle, S-curve, and single track do add a Crawford Notch scene to the Maine & Vermont's collection of New England vignettes.

Critical to the practicality of this

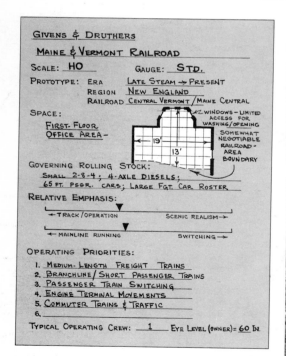

Jim Shaughnessy

Ben Bachman

The HO Maine & Vermont takes as its inspiration the Maine Central and the Central Vermont. (Top right) The reversing loop at Carrabasset furnishes a chance to add a much-condensed version of MeC's spectacular Crawford Notch (New Hampshire) to the M & V. The layout's main yard at Winthrop could resemble this CV and Boston & Maine facility at White River Junction, Vermont (right).

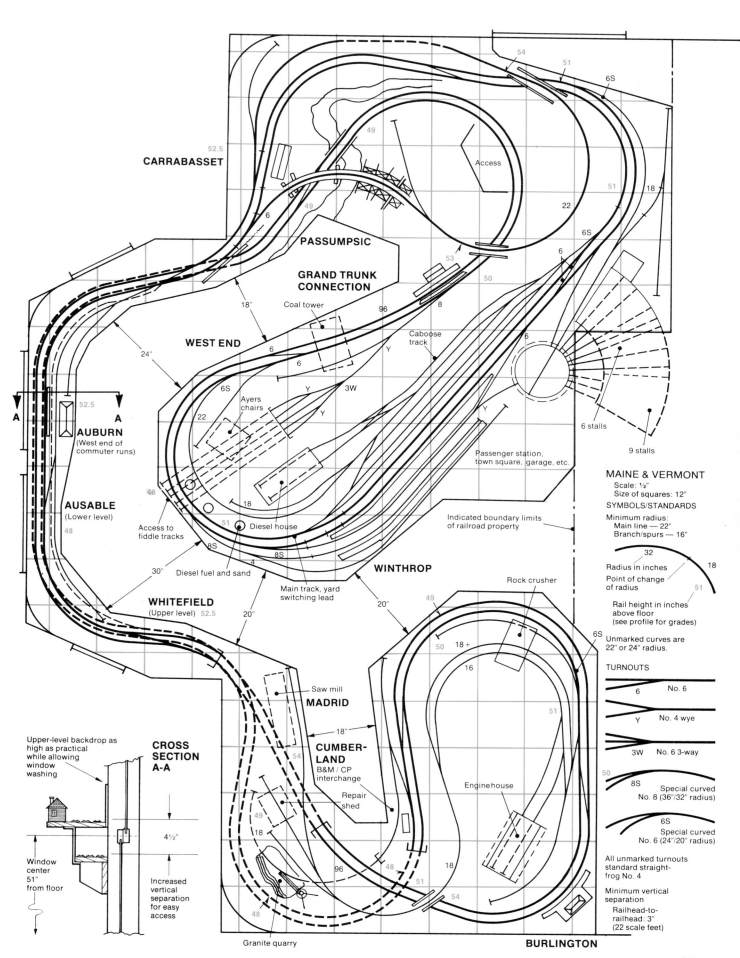

CARRABASSET

52.5

54

51

6S

49

Access

51

18

22

6

PASSUMPSIC

GRAND TRUNK
CONNECTION

53

50

6S

49

6

Coal tower

18"

96

8

6

Caboose
track

WEST END

24"

6

Y

6

Y

3W

6S

Ayers
chairs

Y

Y

22

A   A

52.5

AUBURN
(West end of
commuter runs)

48

Y

18

Passenger station,
town square, garage, etc.

6 stalls

9 stalls

AUSABLE
(Lower level)

48

Access to
fiddle tracks

51

Diesel house

8S

8S

4

Indicated boundary limits
of railroad property

MAINE & VERMONT
Scale: ½"
Size of squares: 12"
SYMBOLS/STANDARDS
Minimum radius:
  Main line — 22"
  Branch/spurs — 16"

32

18

Radius in inches
Point of change
of radius

51

Rail height in inches
above floor
(see profile for grades)

Unmarked curves are
22" or 24" radius.

TURNOUTS

30"

Diesel fuel and sand

Main track, yard
switching lead

WINTHROP

20"

WHITEFIELD
(Upper level) 52.5

20"

Rock crusher

20"

49

6S

50

18 +

16

51

6

No. 6

Y

No. 4 wye

3W

No. 6 3-way

50

8S

Special curved
No. 8 (36"/32" radius)

6S

Special curved
No. 6 (24"/20" radius)

Upper-level backdrop as
high as practical
while allowing
window
washing

**CROSS
SECTION
A-A**

Saw mill

MADRID

18"

**CUMBER-
LAND**
B&M / CP
interchange

Repair
shed

Enginehouse

4½"

54

49

18

All unmarked turnouts
standard straight-
frog No. 4

Minimum vertical
separation
  Railhead-to-
  railhead: 3"
  (22 scale feet)

Window
center
51"
from floor

Increased
vertical
separation
for easy
access

18

96

48

51

18

54

Granite quarry

BURLINGTON

35

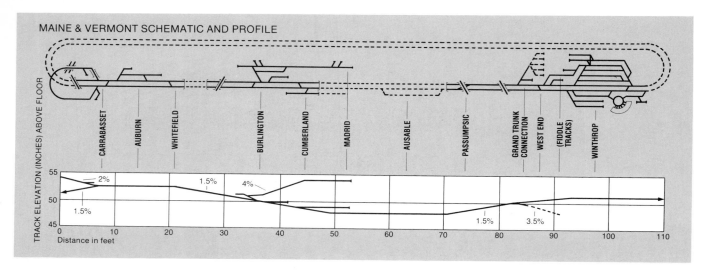

MAINE & VERMONT SCHEMATIC AND PROFILE

space-frugal pike are the curved turn-outs now commercially available. In fact, all trackage on the M & V can be assembled from standard components (in combination with flex-track sections) if desired.

Accommodating an oversize roster. As is so often the case, the roster of rolling stock already at hand and suitable for the territory is larger than can be accommodated on the visible trackage. Adding staging tracks presents a problem: In a plan like this where selection of a reasonably tight minimum radius makes it possible to do a lot of railroading in the space, you do have to accept the fact that fitting layover tracks within the bends is simply not possible.

As a result, some 30 freight cars are to be accommodated in a subterranean, stub-track yard at West End. This underground yard masquerades as the road's Grand Trunk connection, which provides much of the Maine & Vermont's traffic base. A fold-down barrier at the aisle-side end of these tracks makes it easy to fiddle cars on and off the railroad. Trains thus display variety in their makeup commensurate with the wealth of rolling stock on the shelves, and interchange with the rest

of New England and Canada can be much more than a matter of getting back only what was set out last night.

The vertical dimension. Despite the rugged terrain, helper-district operation is not one of the priority goals for this track plan. A good thing, too, because access to those tall windows restricts two segments of the main line (through Ausable on the lower level, Auburn on the top) to a prescribed and constant elevation. The rest of the main line has only short, undulating grades. Nevertheless, the continuous-run main allows freights to be doubled together to a length amply justifying the multi-locomotive consists we think of as typical of northern New England railroading.

Among other compact features that will keep local traffic humming is a quarry company railroad based at Burlington (with its own two-stall engine-house near the junction and a repair shed for its beat-up local-service-only rock cars near the quarry) that brings granite blocks down to the main line and rough stone to the crusher for processing and loading in mainline hoppers. Serving the sawmill at Madrid makes the quarry operation a common carrier.

Those granite blocks that the M & V sets off on the Boston and Maine/Canadian Pacific interchange track at Cumberland return later as empties, courtesy of a fortuitous alignment underneath a granite quarry (with stiff-leg derrick) too deep for the casual observer to see bottom.

Making room for buildings. Already blessed with a spectrum of completed, superdetailed structures, the M & V will quickly achieve a well-equipped, operational status as the track is put in place. However, making room for the proprietor's larger buildings significantly affects the track plan. Diesel fuel and sand facilities are necessarily located on a curved track — which doubles as a bypass thoroughfare for getting a switcher behind an arriving freight so it can begin classifying its cars.

There isn't room for the coaling tower in the approach tracks at the steam engine terminal, so it finds a happy location out on the main line near the West End crossover. This affords the dispatcher the opportunity to either cause or avert disastrous effects on schedule performance by how well he plans the refueling pauses of his trains.

The Pennsylvania Railroad (Richmond, Indiana)

A 17' x 26' attic layout that represents a single busy division point

THE SMALLER the section of railroad we try to model, the closer we can come to reality. Ordinarily, model railroad concepts tend toward representing a lot of railroad in what must be drastically condensed form — we include as long a piece of main line as possible and then append location names to it, suggesting that it stretches tens or hundreds of times as far as it would if expanded in strict scale ratio. While the old joke of labeling one end of a 4' x 8' pike "Grand Central Station" and the other "St. Louis" is pretty well passé, working in enough operational and scenic variety to suit our tastes usually results in stretching reality pretty thin, with Altoona usually one or at the most two scale miles from Pittsburgh.

For once, here's a track plan that picks a time and place with enough railroad action to keep a crew of model railroaders busy all night and reproduces the setting's principal scenic and trackwork features almost literally. The result? For passenger trains, car-

for-car duplication of the operations of a specific timetable in the streamliner era. For motive power, assignments and servicing movements of almost equal accuracy. For freight, a condensation of prototype activity, but by a factor of perhaps three to one in most respects.

Richmond, Indiana, in 1953. By 1953, Pennsylvania Railroad passenger train traffic through Richmond, Indiana, had declined a great deal from its World War Two peak, but most of the through and connecting train and car movements over the six routes passing through this hub were still represented in the public timetable. By limiting the representation of mainline movements beyond yard limits to heading toward or returning from concealed loops via tracks disappearing from the scene in the right general directions, this fairly large HO attic layout portrays the PRR St. Louis line through "Glen" and "Newman" towers with an exceptional degree of fidelity.

Normally in this big a space (which

Frank Barry

GIVENS & DRUTHERS

PENNSYLVANIA RAILROAD - RICHMOND, INDIANA

SCALE: **HO**   GAUGE: **STD.**

PROTOTYPE: ERA _____ **1952** _____
REGION _____ **RICHMOND, IND** _____
RAILROAD _____ **P.R.R. (C&O CONN.)** _____

SPACE:

ATTIC

58" HIGH AT WALL-
CEILING INTERSECTION

—26½'—
17½'   IN

"DISPATCHER'S
CLOSET" —
(PENETRABLE
WALLS)

GOVERNING ROLLING STOCK:
P.R.R. Q-2 4-4-6-4; 85' PASSENGER CARS

RELATIVE EMPHASIS:

◄—— TRACK/OPERATION   SCENIC REALISM ——►

◄—— MAINLINE RUNNING   SWITCHING ——►

OPERATING PRIORITIES:
1. PASSENGER TRAIN SWITCHING (MAIN-LINE TRAINS)
2. LONG FREIGHT-TRAIN OPERATIONS (>20 CARS)
3. TIMETABLE OPERATION
4. ENGINE TERMINAL MOVEMENTS
5. LOCAL FREIGHT OPERATIONS
6.

TYPICAL OPERATING CREW: **2-8**   EYE LEVEL (OWNER)= **67** IN.

Gil Reid

Richmond, Indiana — nothing more, nothing less — is the setting for this purist's layout, and the "Standard Railroad of the World" is its subject matter. Scenes drawn almost literally from the PRR will include (top) the bridge over the Whitewater River near Newman tower, and (above) the train shed at Richmond.

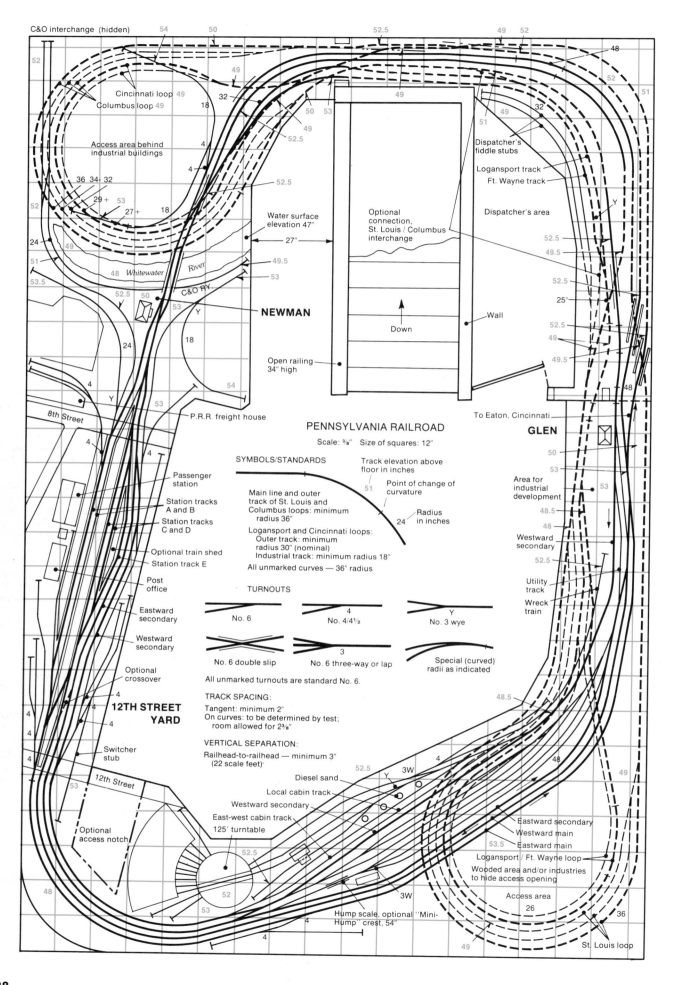

C&O interchange (hidden)

54   50   52.5   49   52

52   48

Cincinnati loop 49
Columbus loop 49   32   52   52

Access area behind   50 53   51
industrial buildings   Dispatcher's
                              4   49   fiddle stubs
                                        52.5   Logansport track
                          4   Ft. Wayne track
36 34 32   Dispatcher's area
        29 +   53
27 +   18
52   Y
24
51
53.5   49   Water surface
                      elevation 47"   52.5
48 Whitewater   River   49.5   49.5
52.5   50   27"
                  C&O RY.   49.5   52.5
            53   Y   53   25°
18   52.5
                                                               49
                              NEWMAN   49.5
24
                                                               48
4   54   Open railing
Y   34" high
8th Street   Down   Wall

                    P.R.R. freight house   Optional
4   connection,   To Eaton, Cincinnati
        53   St. Louis / Columbus
4   interchange   GLEN
                    Passenger
                    station   50
        Station tracks   PENNSYLVANIA RAILROAD   53
        A and B   Scale: ³⁄₈" Size of squares: 12"   Area for
        Station tracks   industrial
        C and D   SYMBOLS/STANDARDS   Track elevation above   development
        Optional train shed   floor in inches   48.5
        Station track E   51   Point of change of   48
        Post   curvature   Westward
        office   Main line and outer   secondary
        Eastward   track of St. Louis and   24   Radius   52.5
        secondary   Columbus loops: minimum   in inches
        Westward   radius 36"   Utility
        secondary   Logansport and Cincinnati loops: track
        Optional   Outer track: minimum   Wreck
        crossover   radius 30" (nominal)   train
                                  Industrial track: minimum radius 18"
4   All unmarked curves — 36" radius
12TH STREET
YARD   TURNOUTS

                                  No. 6   4   Y
4   No. 4/4½   No. 3 wye
4
        Switcher   No. 6 double slip   3
        stub   No. 6 three-way or lap   Special (curved)
4   radii as indicated
        53 12th Street   All unmarked turnouts are standard No. 6.   48.5

        Optional   TRACK SPACING:
        access notch   Tangent: minimum 2"
                                  On curves: to be determined by test;   48
                                  room allowed for 2³⁄₈"
                                                                 4   48
                                  VERTICAL SEPARATION: 49
                                  Railhead-to-railhead — minimum 3"
                                  (22 scale feet)
                    Diesel sand   52.5   Y   3W
                    Local cabin track
                    Westward secondary   Eastward secondary
                    East-west cabin track   Westward main
        125' turntable   Eastward main
48   Logansport / Ft. Wayne loop
                                  52.5   Wooded area and/or industries
                                                                to hide access opening
                    52   Access area
                    53   3W   26
                    Hump scale, optional "Mini-   36
        4   Hump" crest, 54"
4   49   St. Louis loop

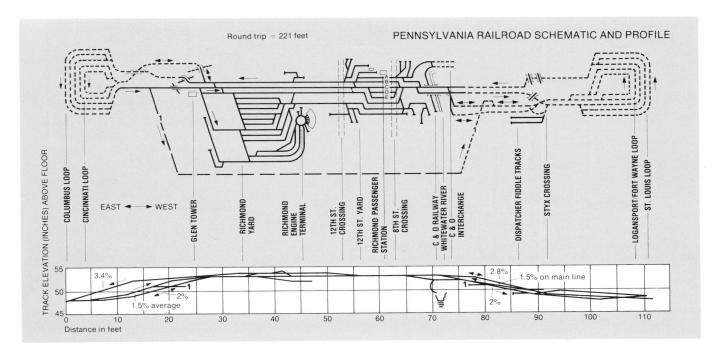

amounts to 5 + x 8 squares after adopting a liberal 36″ minimum radius to accommodate with ease the stiffest PRR locomotives and 85-foot passenger cars) we'd wind the main line back and forth at least a couple of times and claim we were going from Dayton to the east end of Indianapolis, hiding or simply denying the existence of those numerous sharp curves so untypical of this flatland Pennsy territory.

Not so, to meet this man's desires! Only about three-fourths of a single oval of main line is to be visible, a single 48″ curve quietly nestled in one corner of the room connecting two almost-straight diagonals. This arrangement is intended to virtually duplicate the complex downtown Richmond trackage from Newman tower through the passenger station, and to come fairly close to the engine terminal and freight-yard sections west of Glen.

While the trackage between the passenger station and Newman is based directly on PRR track diagrams of the era and the number and designation of station tracks is correct, there's still considerable leeway for interpretation; the Pennsy was continually making minor changes, particularly removing crossovers and rearranging industry tracks. Also, a high, short train shed spanned the platform tracks at the

start of the 1950s but was removed shortly thereafter, giving the proprietor the option of including this interesting structure (but perhaps impairing the view of the trains) or picking a post-shed date — or, for that matter, making a removable shed and shifting dates from time to time.

Multiple return loops. Serving up trains for the Richmond mixing bowl are not only the double tracks east and west on the St. Louis-Columbus main, but also the Cincinnati-Eaton, Ohio, connections from the southeast and the Logansport and Fort Wayne lines from the north (which separate from each other immediately after leaving the St. Louis line at Newman). Since the biggest PRR power didn't operate over these secondary main lines they have been designed with 30″ curves.

Intertwining these loops and their layover sidings to preserve their schematic connecting points, avoid underground conflicts, and maintain reasonable grades so that Indiana-like locomotive assignments will suffice to move full-length passenger trains will require careful construction, particularly in the area behind the stairwell.

A principal option in the schematic is the continuous-run mainline bypass (via the hidden St. Louis-Columbus interchange) which will allow a train to

make successive mainline journeys in the same direction. Without the bypass anything going to St. Louis must return eastward on the same line; with it, a limited roster can still be used to run properly recognizable extra sections of some of the Pennsy's famous long name trains.

Freight trackage, with eastbound and westbound secondary tracks paralleling the passenger mains from Glen to Newman, is authentic; the classification yard between them is of course much condensed. The mini-hump simulates the prototype operation, a busy yard which never did rate retarders. Coal traffic was not a major item in this territory, so running mainline freights back and forth without regard to the loaded or empty condition of the open-tops is not a serious affront to reality.

With the coming of Penn Central and the ultimate diversion of through traffic in this territory to former New York Central lines, Richmond's status as a hub whose importance far exceeded that typical of a town of its size and industrial output was lost. In this strictly "Standard Railroad of the World" HO reincarnation, however, crews at Richmond can continue to shuffle the Tuscan red cars and watch the double-headed K4s come and go.

The Denver & Rio Grande Western (On3) and the Union Pacific (HO)

Two overlapping but visually separate layouts sharing a common space

MIX On3 and HO in the same layout? No, that's not the objective here — and undoubtedly just as well, since the HO in this case is big-time, late steam era railroading which wouldn't make an appropriate background for the narrow gauge, and putting the HO trains in front of those big On3 models would certainly kill the overall effect.

What this proprietor desires is a two-layout arrangement in a single basement, sharing space wherever possible, that will allow the owner to indulge two urges which stubbornly resist giving way to each other. The On3 urge is the businesslike quaintness of the final days of narrow gauge steam in a scale big enough to be fully appreciated, and the other is the ultimate appeal of steam's finest hour in the form of standard gauge 4-12-2s, Big Boys, and Rio Grande L-131s (and maybe a gas turbine or two) hauling long mainline trains in HO. Fortunately, the space available is a *big* basement, 22' x 43'.

Designed for an experienced modeler. This is not a "starter" layout, and the builder has already done enough operating in both scales to know that

such exotica as "reverted" return loops, with their requirement that trains make a backing move to get into position for a return trip, will work reliably if alignment, trackwork, and rolling stock are all first-class.

To handle the biggest-of-its-type rolling stock in both late-steam HO and On3 D & RGW narrow gauge it turns out that a common minimum mainline radius of 42" should be about right — liberal to the point of reliably accommodating locomotive driver wheelbases and trailing truck swiveling with minimum compromise to prototype dimensions and details, yet leaving the space equivalent to 5½ x 10½ squares, which by now we all know is compatible with a highly realistic walk-in design.

Achieving realism while incorporating two basically incompatible scales requires that they not share the same scene at any point, but we need not separate them by a wall. At some points, particularly along the wall at Charango, the big little trains will be visible on one side of the aisle, across from the little big ones. Since you'll generally be looking directly at one or the other

when anything interesting is going on, the fact that eyes in the back of your head could see something clashing in time or size isn't worth worrying about.

Dividing the space. The space has to be divided between the two scales, though. Should the division be generally crosswise or lengthwise in the room? Playing with the squares shows that only a lengthwise division will provide a satisfactorily long yard for the HO and the generally sweeping curves and long tangents typical of Big Boy and 4-12-2 country. We end up with an area for the HO railroad in one corner of the basement equivalent to

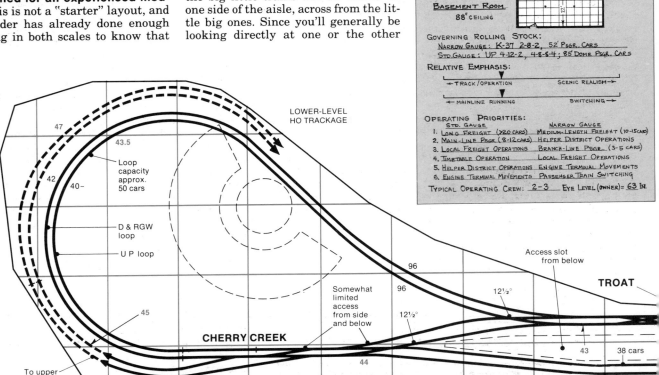

GIVENS & DRUTHERS

DENVER & RIO GRANDE WESTERN / UNION PACIFIC

SCALE: O AND HO   GAUGE: 3 FT. / STD.

PROTOTYPE: ERA   LATE STEAM
REGION   COLORADO ROCKIES
RAILROAD   D&RGW NARROW GA./UP, D&RGW STD.GA.

SPACE:

BASEMENT ROOM
88" CEILING

GOVERNING ROLLING STOCK:
NARROW GAUGE: K-37 2-8-2, 52' PSGR. CARS
STD.GAUGE: UP 4-12-2, 4-8-8-4; 85' DOME PSGR. CARS

RELATIVE EMPHASIS:
←TRACK/OPERATION   SCENIC REALISM→
←MAINLINE RUNNING   SWITCHING→

OPERATING PRIORITIES:
STD. GAUGE   NARROW GAUGE
1. LONG FREIGHT (>20 CARS)   MEDIUM-LENGTH FREIGHT (10-15 CARS)
2. MAIN-LINE PSGR. (8-12 CARS)   HELPER DISTRICT OPERATIONS
3. LOCAL FREIGHT OPERATIONS   BRANCH-LINE PSGR. (3-5 CARS)
4. TIMETABLE OPERATION   LOCAL FREIGHT OPERATIONS
5. HELPER DISTRICT OPERATIONS   ENGINE TERMINAL MOVEMENTS
6. ENGINE TERMINAL MOVEMENTS   PASSENGER TRAIN SWITCHING
TYPICAL OPERATING CREW: 2-3   EYE LEVEL (OWNER) = 63 IN.

LOWER-LEVEL HO TRACKAGE

47

43.5

Loop capacity approx. 50 cars

42

40-

D & RGW loop

U P loop

45

96

96

12½°

THROAT

Access slot from below

12½°

Somewhat limited access from side and below

12½°

CHERRY CREEK

43

38 cars

44

To upper level

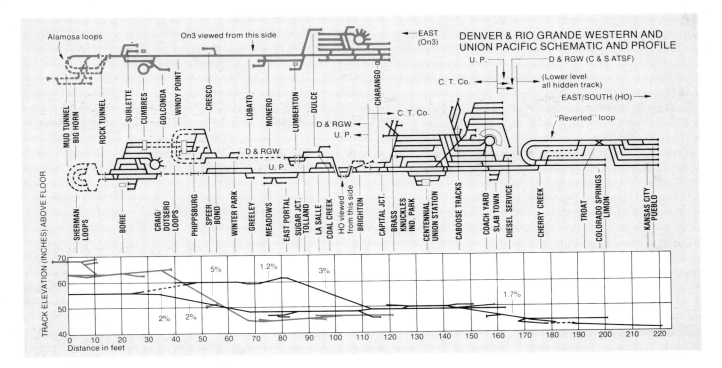

DENVER & RIO GRANDE WESTERN AND
UNION PACIFIC SCHEMATIC AND PROFILE

about 4 x 8 squares, with the L-shaped On3 railroad taking its place along one side and one end. By overlapping the two layouts at various points with only the top one visible, the whole can be greater than the sum of the parts so far as space efficiency is concerned.

There isn't room in the lower left corner of the room for a return bend in either scale without impinging on the doorway. Moving the bend away from the corner far enough for comfortable entry for man and plywood would be a considerable waste, so the On3 with its properly less frenetic traffic is confined to an out-and-back, terminal-to-loop schematic. The stub at Charango, made to look like a continuing main line, makes good use of the dead-end space.

The choice of a section of the Rio Grande's latter-day narrow gauge as the prototype is an obvious one — the line over Cumbres Pass has the traffic, the 4 percent grade, the scenery, and it's a logical home base for the rotary snowplow and other superdetailed On3 maintenance-of-way equipment which is a major facet of this model railroad and deserves a realistic display.

The narrow gauge comes out too straight! In developing the On3 portion of the plan we run into a rare problem — the model tends to come out straighter than the prototype's Tanglefoot Curve and other contorted alignments. With the cooperation of the HO

in wriggling its aisleways, though, the principal grade representing the west side of Cumbres from Lobato Trestle up past Windy Point to the summit (where there is room for a Marshall Pass-type turntable rather than the prototype's wye in a snowshed) has enough curvature for realistic scenes.

The HO railroad can most realistically accommodate the motive power of interest to the proprietor by representing some territory where the UP and D & RGW (standard gauge) are neighbors; essentially, this means Denver or Salt Lake City/Ogden. We pick the former, calling a thinly disguised Denver "Centennial City" so that some of our lines may run off in somewhat non-prototypical relative directions.

This ruse allows Santa Fe, Colorado & Southern (Burlington), and Rock Island motive power to appear on the scene, and by having our UP head for Kansas out of the south end of the Den . . . oops, Centennial Union Station a number of through-train routings are reasonably prototypical and make good use of the turnaround and layover capacity of the reverted loop at the east and south end of the line.

Accommodation and access. As you'd expect for a railroad this big, dozens of locomotives and hundreds of cars must be accommodated. Many will have to be on shelves, but the reverted-loop tail tracks with layover capacity of

about 275 cars go a long way toward easing the situation. To ease the access problems of this secluded (if not completely hidden) trackage, the loop itself is pitched at a 1.7 percent grade, which should pose no problem for the big motive power and allows from 5″ to 7″ between the stubs and the Centennial yard above. Thin-deck construction is required, but with the access slots indicated the situation should be workable.

The important Cherry Creek crossovers have limited access from below, enough for recovering from operating incidents but not for what could conceivably happen over the years to the trackwork, so a "dire emergency" hatch is located above. At all points in this two-level area the track arrangement keeps turnouts as close to the open edges as possible; the reverted-loop turnouts where backing movements will be routine are arranged so trains will take the straight leg — a useful percentage play.

Fast and loose geography. Out on the main lines of the standard gauge Rio Grande and UP the nature and sequence of stations is only generally reminiscent of reality — I have shamelessly moved the UP's big westbound hill from Wyoming southeastward into Colorado so that the Challengers and Big Boys will have a chance to use their tractive effort, and while the *California Zephyr* can take the proper

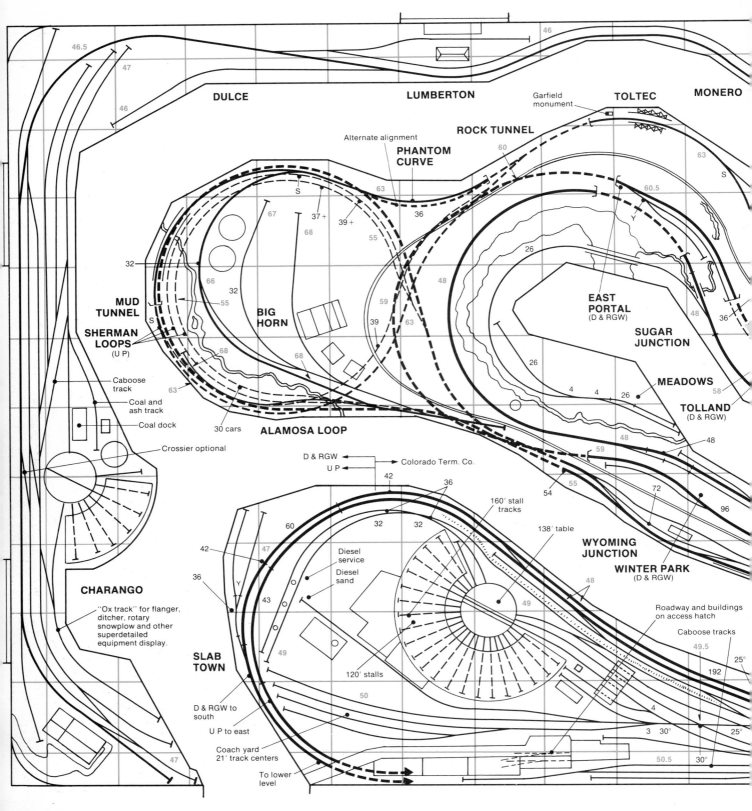

DULCE   LUMBERTON   Garfield monument   TOLTEC   MONERO

46.5   47   46

ROCK TUNNEL

Alternate alignment
PHANTOM
CURVE

60   63   S

63   60.5   Y

36

67   37 +   39 +   55   68   26   EAST
PORTAL
(D & RGW)

32   66   32   55   48   59   SUGAR
JUNCTION

MUD
TUNNEL   BIG
HORN   39   63   26   48   36

SHERMAN
LOOPS
(U P)   S   26   4   4   26   MEADOWS   58

Caboose track   68   TOLLAND
(D & RGW)

Coal and ash track   63   68

Coal dock   30 cars   48   48

ALAMOSA LOOP   59

Crossier optional   D & RGW   Colorado Term. Co.   55   54   72

U P   42   36   96

42   160' stall
tracks   WYOMING
JUNCTION

60   32   32   138' table   48   WINTER PARK
(D & RGW)

42   47   Diesel
service   Roadway and buildings
on access hatch

36   Y   Diesel
sand   Caboose tracks

43   49   49.5   25°

CHARANGO   49   192   25°

"Ox track" for flanger,
ditcher, rotary
snowplow and other
superdetailed
equipment display.   120' stalls   50   4

SLAB
TOWN   3   30°   25°

D & RGW to
south   50.5   30°

U P to east

Coach yard
21' track centers

To lower
level

left-hand track at Bond, it will have to sneak back off the old Moffat Road on its eastbound journey. Well, some of the year this is after dark, anyway!

The mighty Moffat Tunnel is barely long enough to temporarily hide a 30-car train, but with the indicated grades the vertical separation between the Rio Grande and UP — up to a foot in places — does help to create a feeling that they are going different places

even if they must be somewhat intertwined horizontally.

This intertwining provides the opportunity for substantial (25 cars or so) coal traffic on an empties in/loads out basis between Phippsburg on the Moffat and a power plant on the UP at Borie, about a 200' trip via Centennial City.

Geographical realities have also been bent considerably in locating spurs to make good use of idle space and to pro-

vide healthy levels of local freight activity. The cattle and oil originating area at Big Horn on the narrow gauge isn't strictly prototypical, but the tonnage will do a lot for realistic traffic patterns on the Cumbres line, and the long spur at Meadows on the UP can help provide the feel of the sugar beet country, even given the presence of the Continental Divide only a couple of feet away on the Rio Grande.

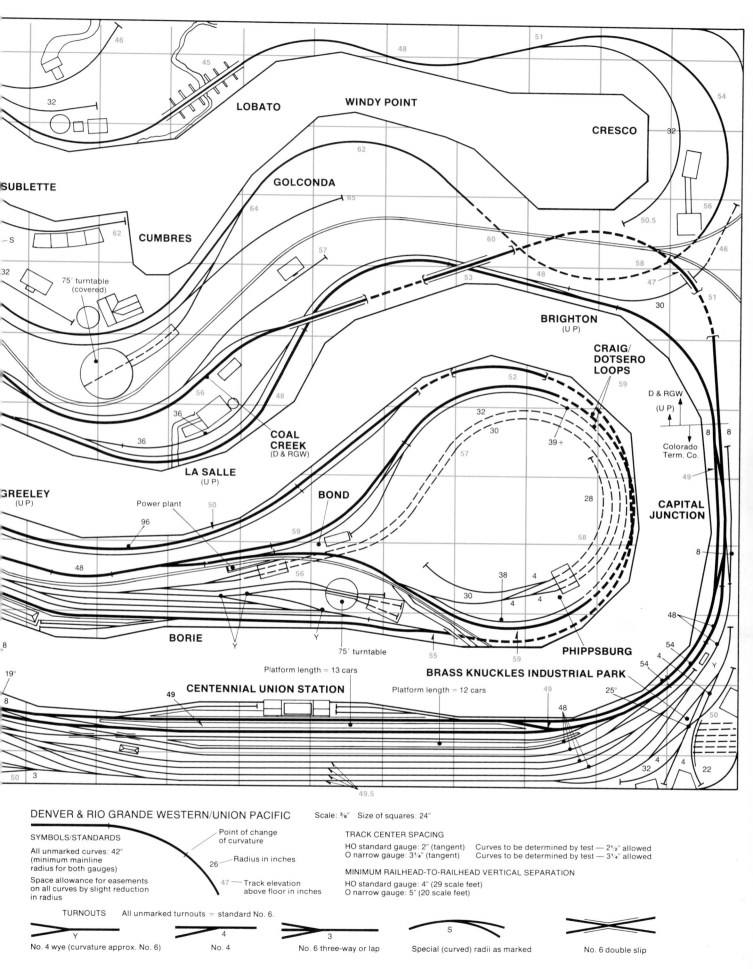

46

45

32

48

51

54

LOBATO

WINDY POINT

CRESCO

32

SUBLETTE

62

65

64

62

50.5

56

– S

CUMBRES

57

60

58

46

53

48

47

51

75' turntable
(covered)

32

56

48

30

BRIGHTON
(U P)

52

59

CRAIG/
DOTSERO
LOOPS

32

36

30

39 +

D & RGW
(U P)

36

36

COAL
CREEK
(D & RGW)

57

28

58

Colorado
Term. Co.

8

8

LA SALLE
(U P)

49

BOND

GREELEY
(U P)

Power plant

50

CAPITAL
JUNCTION

96

59

58

8

48

38

4

48

30

4

4

54

BORIE

Y

Y

75' turntable

55

59

PHIPPSBURG

4

54

Platform length = 13 cars

BRASS KNUCKLES INDUSTRIAL PARK

25°

19°

CENTENNIAL UNION STATION

Platform length = 12 cars

49

48

8

49

48

50

32

4

22

50

3

49.5

DENVER & RIO GRANDE WESTERN/UNION PACIFIC

Scale: ³⁄₈″   Size of squares: 24″

SYMBOLS/STANDARDS

All unmarked curves: 42″
(minimum mainline
radius for both gauges)

Space allowance for easements
on all curves by slight reduction
in radius

Point of change
of curvature

26 — Radius in inches

47 — Track elevation
above floor in inches

TRACK CENTER SPACING

HO standard gauge: 2″ (tangent)   Curves to be determined by test — 2½″ allowed
O narrow gauge: 3¼″ (tangent)   Curves to be determined by test — 3¼″ allowed

MINIMUM RAILHEAD-TO-RAILHEAD VERTICAL SEPARATION

HO standard gauge: 4″ (29 scale feet)
O narrow gauge: 5″ (20 scale feet)

TURNOUTS   All unmarked turnouts = standard No. 6.

Y

No. 4 wye (curvature approx. No. 6)

4

No. 4

3

No. 6 three-way or lap

S

Special (curved) radii as marked

No. 6 double slip

The Union Terminal Railroad

Heavy-duty HO railroading in minimum space, thanks to multilayer construction

IT MAY BE HARD for those who are themselves or are acquainted with "slobberin' Pennsy fans" to realize, but there actually are some model railroaders who like both Pennsylvania Railroad and New York Central System steam power — to the extent that they must have some of each operating on their pikes. Such is the case here, where the newest, finest, and most rigid examples of these majestic locomotives must somehow do their thing in a modest 7' x 12' basement alcove.

Dual standards. In an effort to handle HO gauge Niagaras and Pennsy J-1 2-10-4s in some fashion without also limiting Hudsons, K4s, and I1s to strictly round-and-round operation, dual standards are established: 30" minimum radius over at least one continuous route for the long-wheelbase power, 22" minimum (with easements) for the medium-size engines and their passenger cars, accepting as inevitable the re-

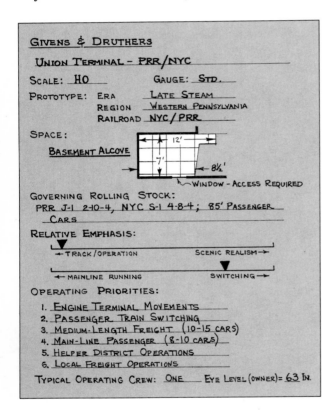

GIVENS & DRUTHERS

UNION TERMINAL - PRR/NYC

SCALE: HO   GAUGE: STD.

PROTOTYPE: ERA   LATE STEAM
           REGION WESTERN PENNSYLVANIA
           RAILROAD NYC/PRR

SPACE:
BASEMENT ALCOVE [12', 7', 8½', WINDOW - ACCESS REQUIRED]

GOVERNING ROLLING STOCK:
PRR J-1 2-10-4, NYC S-1 4-8-4; 85' PASSENGER CARS

RELATIVE EMPHASIS:
◄—TRACK/OPERATION   SCENIC REALISM—►
◄—MAINLINE RUNNING   SWITCHING—►

OPERATING PRIORITIES:
1. ENGINE TERMINAL MOVEMENTS
2. PASSENGER TRAIN SWITCHING
3. MEDIUM-LENGTH FREIGHT (10-15 CARS)
4. MAIN-LINE PASSENGER (8-10 CARS)
5. HELPER DISTRICT OPERATIONS
6. LOCAL FREIGHT OPERATIONS

TYPICAL OPERATING CREW: ONE   EYE LEVEL (OWNER)= 63 IN.

New York Central

There won't be room to model the immense building, but equipment on the Union Terminal will be reminiscent of PRR and NYC operations at Buffalo's Central Terminal.

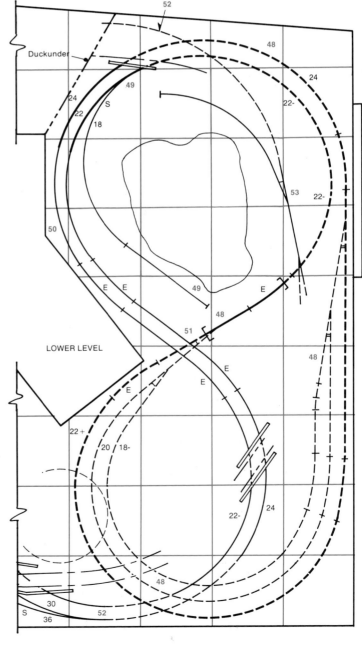

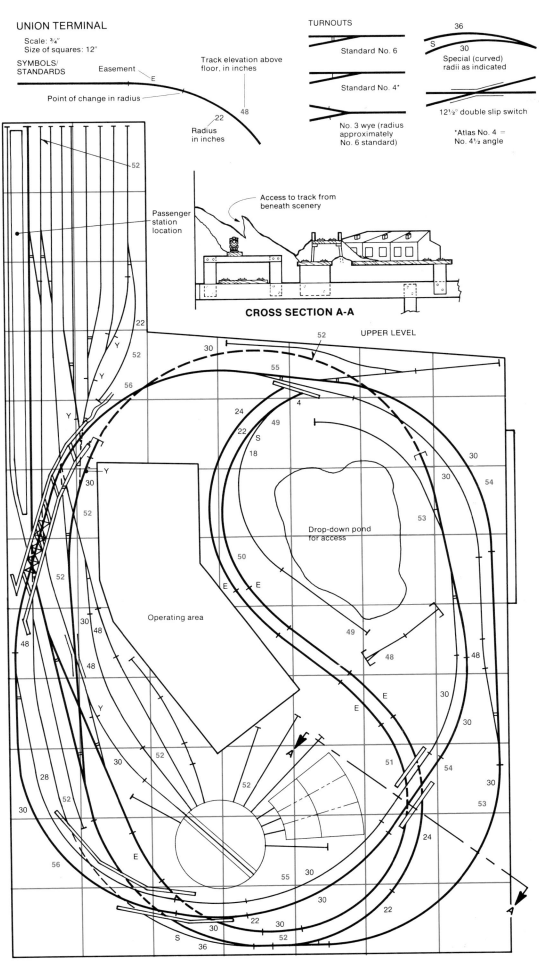

UNION TERMINAL

Scale: ¾"
Size of squares: 12"

SYMBOLS/
STANDARDS

Easement

E

Point of change in radius

Track elevation above
floor, in inches

48

22

Radius
in inches

TURNOUTS

Standard No. 6

Standard No. 4*

No. 3 wye (radius
approximately
No. 6 standard)

36

S

30

Special (curved)
radii as indicated

12½° double slip switch

*Atlas No. 4 =
No. 4½ angle

MINIMUM RADIUS:
Upper level main line = 30"
Lower level "down and
back" — 22" with
easements
Industry tracks, etc. — 18"

MINIMUM TRACK-
CENTER SPACING

On tangent track — 2"
On curves — to be deter-
mined by test; space
allowed for 2½" centers

MINIMUM
VERTICAL SEPARATION

Railhead-to-railhead =
3" (22 scale feet)

Passenger
station
location

Access to track from
beneath scenery

CROSS SECTION A-A

UPPER LEVEL

Drop-down pond
for access

Operating area

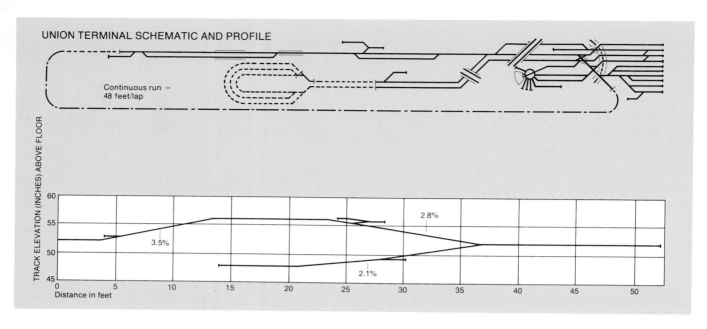

UNION TERMINAL SCHEMATIC AND PROFILE

Continuous run = 48 feet/lap

TRACK ELEVATION (INCHES) ABOVE FLOOR

3.5%

2.8%

2.1%

Distance in feet

sulting somewhat ungainly appearance.

On this basis, the area available works out to be equivalent to about 3 x 4 squares, with a short panhandle which obviously must end up as a stub terminal. Justifying the common presence of the rival classes of power needs only that we assume a Union Terminal operation, for which several prototypes exist. Buffalo is one example where almost purely NYC/PRR operations were the rule, though we certainly won't have room to represent the NYC's through operations in the huge Buffalo Central Terminal.

A surprising amount of operation. What's possible? For the equipment that requires the large radius all we can have is a simple oval in an up-and-over, twice-around expansion. This will allow one fairly long train (pieced together by repeated dips into the short attached stub trackage) to go through its paces at a time. Local trains in the

opposite direction will provide operating interest as long as they are short enough to fit into the two passing tracks for which room can be found.

Smaller but more flexible locomotives will haul short trains from the terminal in an out, down, and back fashion, traversing a scenic S-curve in the process and hiding out in subterranean layover sidings on the lower deck. Grades are steep, but not troublesome for such limited tonnage.

Operation and most viewing will be from a comfortable area overlooking both the yard throat and the relatively ample engine service facilities. The engine terminal area meets the proprietor's top-priority requirement of displaying those elegant iron horses in an environment which can be superdetailed to a fine degree. Getting in there to see those goodies, of course, means a duckunder.

Adding to the panhandle. In the

particular situation for which this plan was developed the length of the panhandle portion of the layout had to be severely restricted. Each additional foot which can be made available — if need be on a drop leaf or lift-out section — will expand the operational capabilities of the entire layout enormously.

Putting a double slip switch directly under a bridge is nothing you like to do, but it is essential in this case and undeniably sincere since solving tough space problems is what double slips are used for in prototype throats. Fortunately, HO gaugers now have good curved turnouts available in prefabricated form; the one at the left end of this plan is absolutely essential to the concept of the whole railroad.

Don't compare a track plan like the Union Terminal to one of the big ones and feel bad — instead, compare it to those rows of big locomotives sitting on shelves and feel *good*!

The Chicago & North Western Railroad

A double-deck, continuous-run, garage layout based on a towering bridge on a flatland railroad

THE CHICAGO & NORTH Western is the most typical of the "granger" railroads serving the non-mountainous and enormously productive agricultural heartland of the United States. In spite of its overall flatland character, the North Western has one whopper of a high bridge set amid the rolling landscape of Iowa, and that bridge sets the theme of this plan.

The Kate Shelley Bridge that carries the C & NW's double-track Chicago-Omaha main line straight across the valley of the Des Moines River near Boone, Iowa, is a towering steel trestle with a central truss span over the river itself. The structure is named for a real-life heroine who crawled across the old Des Moines River bridge in a storm to warn the North Western station agent of a trestle washout farther down the line, thereby preventing a disastrous passenger-train wreck. In our plan's condensed but still impressive HO representation, the big bridge is 75 inches long and 15 inches high.

The viaduct was completed in 1900 to replace the winding, steeply graded original line that required through trains to descend into the valley and then climb out again. Together with the nearby division point at Boone and the remnant of the low line for local traffic, the big bridge helps to crowd a lot of vertical scenic variation and railroading activity into a highly compact, 12' x 16' area, in this case a single-car garage.

Of course, there's a price to be paid to include the bridge, mainline passenger traffic, and all the proprietor's other druthers in such a compact setting. Here the tariff is moderately sophisticated construction, including a two-turn helix.

Twice around a doughnut. The minimum mainline curvature suitable for those Overland Route limiteds in HO is 28", and the space available works out to 3 x 6 squares. That immediately jells the basic plan, because a continuous run is essential for reasonably long passenger consists and there is simply no form of walk-in arrangement that will fit.

Once you duck into the middle of the doughnut layout from that side entrance, though, you can do a lot of railroading before next flexing your sacroiliac (if the phone doesn't ring). The almost-inevitable twice-around oval will provide reasonably comfortable conditions for both operating and viewing, and enough of a run to let the markers get well out of sight before the headlight next looms into the scene.

The scenic highlight of the model is to be the way the big bridge towers over the branch and its low-level, somewhat rickety crossing of the same river, so we want to do everything possible to emphasize this disparity. The prototype's 185' height scales out to 25½" in HO, and even cutting this in half still means that we have to cheat and use a helix to get our branch that far down in practical fashion. Once it's down there, vertical spacing between railheads is enough for two-level scenic treatment of the far end of the branch.

Incidentally, you'll note that the plan includes no finished schematic or profile; the proprietor expressed no desire for either. As math texts used to say, "the proof is left to the student."

Filling in the details. The details of this design are important in suppress-

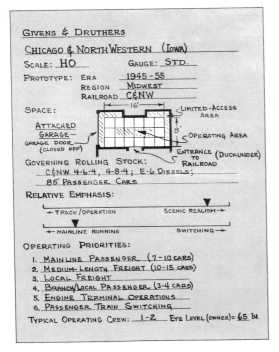

GIVENS & DRUTHERS

CHICAGO & NORTH WESTERN (IOWA)

SCALE: HO   GAUGE: STD.

PROTOTYPE: ERA   1945 - 55
           REGION   MIDWEST
           RAILROAD C&NW

SPACE: ← LIMITED-ACCESS
                               AREA
ATTACHED
GARAGE —   ← OPERATING AREA
GARAGE DOOR
(CLOSED OFF)   ← ENTRANCE (DUCKUNDER)
                              TO
                              RAILROAD

GOVERNING ROLLING STOCK:
   C&NW 4-6-4, 4-8-4; E-6 DIESELS;
   85' PASSENGER CARS

RELATIVE EMPHASIS:

← TRACK/OPERATION   SCENIC REALISM →

← MAINLINE RUNNING   SWITCHING →

OPERATING PRIORITIES:
   1. MAINLINE PASSENGER (7-10 CARS)
   2. MEDIUM-LENGTH FREIGHT (10-15 CARS)
   3. LOCAL FREIGHT
   4. BRANCH/LOCAL PASSENGER (3-4 CARS)
   5. ENGINE TERMINAL OPERATIONS
   6. PASSENGER TRAIN SWITCHING

TYPICAL OPERATING CREW: 1-2   EYE LEVEL (OWNER)= 65 IN.

Henry J. McCord

The double-tracked Boone Viaduct carries the Chicago & North Western's main line straight across the valley of the Des Moines River near Boone, Iowa.

ing the twice-around look of the main line, and in making it clear that this is the North Western in Iowa and not another model railroad through the mountains. Taking the second lap up and over the first is preferable to a crossing at grade in this instance, as the constant clickety-clack over frogs that shouldn't be there would be more disturbing than the unprototypical (but moderate for a model railroad) grades required to get one lap over the other.

Some of the most crucial details are:

• Mainline operation is left-handed as befits the North Western. The effects of this on the track arrangement show up in such matters as the direction in which most industry spurs are attached to the main.

• Trees are useful for hiding tracks and trains at various points, either by themselves or in combination with buildings or modest terraces in the terrain. The effectiveness of this technique depends on having the main line up near eye level, which of course is also highly desirable to ease the stooping needed to enter the operating area.

• All turnouts on the railroad are accessible, but some of the semi-hidden crossovers are accessible only from end and rear access slots which can be reached only via a fairly uncomfortable under-the-layout crawl. The heavily used yard turnouts, where derailments are most likely to occur, are up front and close to the operating area.

• An effective (that is, subtle) transition between single-level and two-level scenery is achieved at the approach to Grand Junction on the branch by hiding the joint with a tall building which doubles as a grain elevator down below and a feed mill on the upper level in "downtown" Ogden.

• As a rural division point, Boone's passenger station is primarily a place for servicing long trains and has only limited amenities for the predominantly pass-holding residents likely to begin or end journeys there. That rationale takes care of the absence of umbrella sheds over the platforms, which just happens to be better for showing off the trains.

• The freight yard at Boone is considerably smaller than would be typical of even a secondary division point, but it's all that fits. Its operations will there-

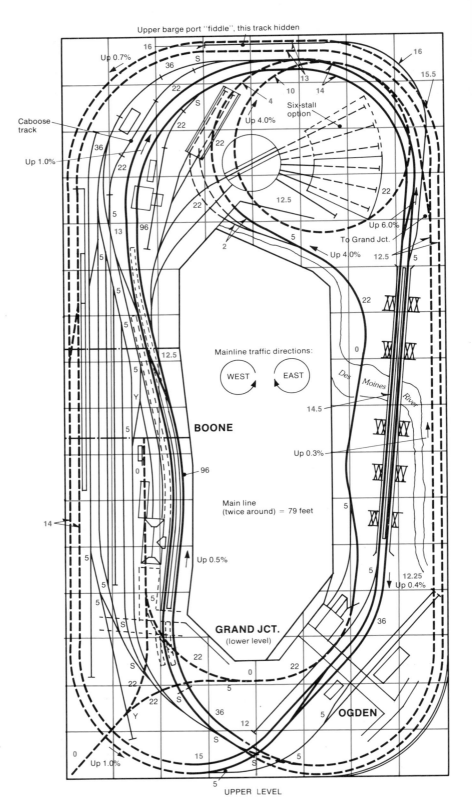

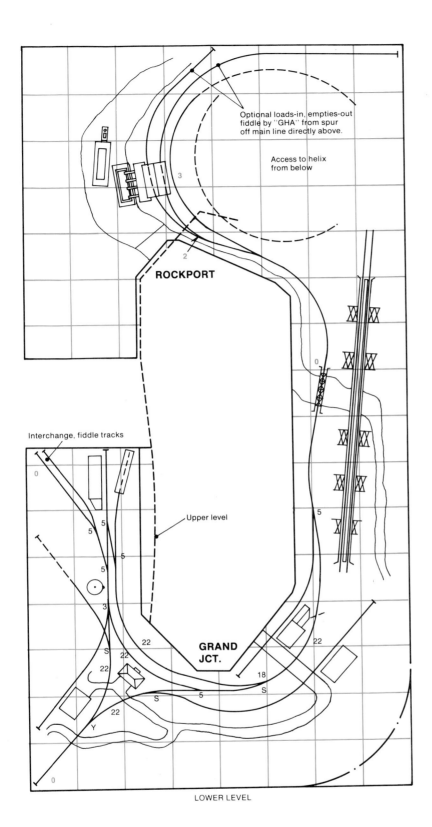

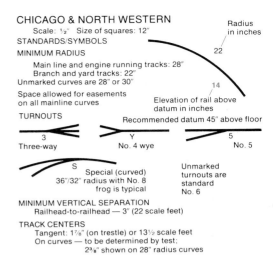

ROCKPORT

Optional loads-in, empties-out
fiddle by "GHA" from spur
off main line directly above.

Access to helix
from below

Interchange, fiddle tracks

Upper level

GRAND
JCT.

LOWER LEVEL

CHICAGO & NORTH WESTERN

Scale: ½"   Size of squares: 12"

STANDARDS/SYMBOLS

MINIMUM RADIUS

Main line and engine running tracks: 28"
Branch and yard tracks: 22"
Unmarked curves are 28" or 30"

Space allowed for easements
on all mainline curves

Radius
in inches
22

Elevation of rail above
datum in inches

Recommended datum 45" above floor

TURNOUTS

3 — Three-way   Y — No. 4 wye   5 — No. 5

S — Special (curved)
36"/32" radius with No. 8
frog is typical

Unmarked
turnouts are
standard
No. 6

MINIMUM VERTICAL SEPARATION
Railhead-to-railhead — 3" (22 scale feet)

TRACK CENTERS
Tangent: 1⅞" (on trestle) or 13½ scale feet
On curves — to be determined by test;
2⅜" shown on 28" radius curves

fore be limited to exchanging cars between through freights and locals working the main line and branch. There is, however, one facility large enough to give a big-time flavor to the yard: At one spotting the icing station can re-ice half the reefers of a model-length eastbound perishable train.

● As befits the era, both steam and diesel facilities are included in an engine terminal that's somewhat oversize in proportion to the rest of the railroad. Location of the coaling station is optional; either the main line or the roundhouse lead is appropriate.

An interesting optional feature is the barge-loading terminal on the branch at Rockport, destination for the considerable gravel traffic out of a quarry spur on the main line. This is strictly unprototypical as the real C & NW does no such business on the banks of the Des Moines, but operationally it could be intriguing. Loads-east/empties-west movement would be simulated by a concealed GHA (Giant Hand Action) fiddle operation between the "around the curve" tails of the Rockport spurs and the Upper Bargeport spur just above.

As ordered, this plan gives first priority to the bridge scene and its mainline traffic. Even given that emphasis, there's still more than a little play value — or "operating interest," if you prefer — in case you ever tire of watching *City* streamliners and blocks of reefers sailing over the valley of the Des Moines.

The Rio Grande Southern Railroad

A sit-in HOn3 layout to be built in a small room

GIVENS & DRUTHERS

RIO GRANDE SOUTHERN

SCALE: **HO**   GAUGE: **n3**

PROTOTYPE: ERA   LATE STEAM
          REGION   S.W. COLORADO
          RAILROAD   R.G.S.

SPACE: 8'8" x 6'8" ROOM —
          DOOR RE-HUNG TO
          SWING OUT. NO
          OTHER RESTRICTIONS...

GOVERNING ROLLING STOCK:
   K-36 2-8-2; 48' PASSENGER CARS (MARGIN
   OF SAFETY BEYOND K-27, 39' CARS IN REGULAR SERVICE)

RELATIVE EMPHASIS:

   ▼
   ├── TRACK/OPERATION   SCENIC REALISM ──►

              ▼
   ◄── MAINLINE RUNNING   SWITCHING ──►

OPERATING PRIORITIES:
   1. BRANCH-LINE/SHORT PASSENGER (3-4 CARS)
   2. LOCAL FREIGHT OPERATION
   3. HELPER-DISTRICT OPERATIONS
   4. ENGINE TERMINAL MOVEMENTS
   5.
   6.

TYPICAL OPERATING CREW: ONE   EYE LEVEL (OWNER)= 66 IN.

NO DOUBT ABOUT IT — this railroad is going to fall into the "little gem" category. Given rigid walls enclosing a 6' 8" x 8' 8" space and the proprietor's desire to emphasize realistic scenes rather than a complete jumble of track, the plan is going to be simple enough to permit superdetailing the whole thing — and that includes track, bridges, structures, rolling stock, lighting, sound effects, the works!

Achieving vertical separation. Even with the door to the room rehung to swing outward, there's not going to be room to use a two-level design in a scenically plausible arrangement — you could get up to an upper deck with a helix, but there would be no way to get back down without real crowding. What comes to the rescue is the prototype: The choice of the Rio Grande Southern

is unbeatable. RGS mainline grades, which started at a stiff 2.5 percent and increased to 4 percent on the approaches to Dallas Divide (along with many 24-degree curves — that's a 31" radius in HO scale), were just starters. Some of the mine branches were *steep!* So, choosing to model the RGS does legitimately make possible the maximum vertical separation between tracks which simply can't be kept as far apart in the horizontal direction as realism would otherwise demand.

Our latter-day HOn3 RGS comes with the requirement for motive power as big as a K-27 Mikado, so a 20" minimum mainline radius (with easements) is appropriate. That's tight, but not so skimpy as to require disfiguring modifications to achieve reliable operation with the big engine. As a result, the

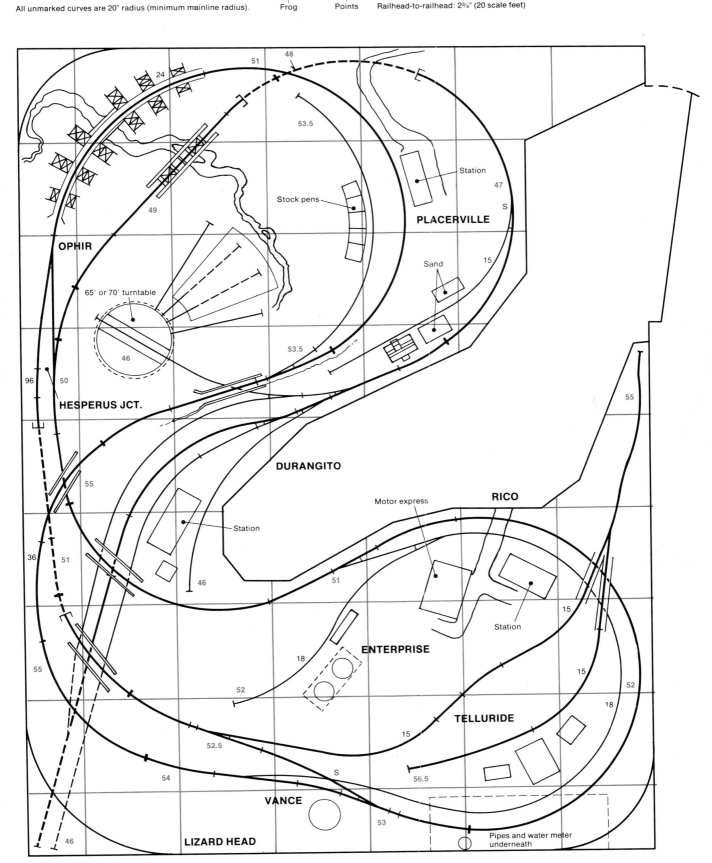

RIO GRANDE SOUTHERN
SYMBOLS/STANDARDS

Point of tangent

Point of transition:
easement to circular curve

Radius of curve in inches

All unmarked curves are 20″ radius (minimum mainline radius).

Scale: 1″
Size of squares: 12″

Rail elevation
above floor
in inches

TURNOUTS

Special curved
radii as indicated

Frog   Points

All unmarked turnouts
are No. 6.

TRACK CENTERS
Tangent: 1¾″ (12+ scale feet)
Curves: to be determined by test to suit equipment;
        2″ (14½ scale feet) allowed on plan

MINIMUM VERTICAL SEPARATION
Railhead-to-railhead: 2¾″ (20 scale feet)

24
48
24

51   48
53.5
Station
47
S

Stock pens
PLACERVILLE
Sand
15

OPHIR
49

65′ or 70′ turntable
46
53.5

96   50
HESPERUS JCT.
55

DURANGITO

Motor express   RICO
Station
55
51
36   51
46
51
Station
15

ENTERPRISE
18
55
52
TELLURIDE
15
15
52
18

52.5
54
S
VANCE
53
56.5
15

LIZARD HEAD
46
Pipes and water meter
underneath

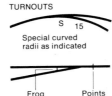
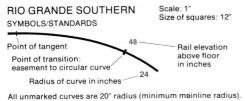

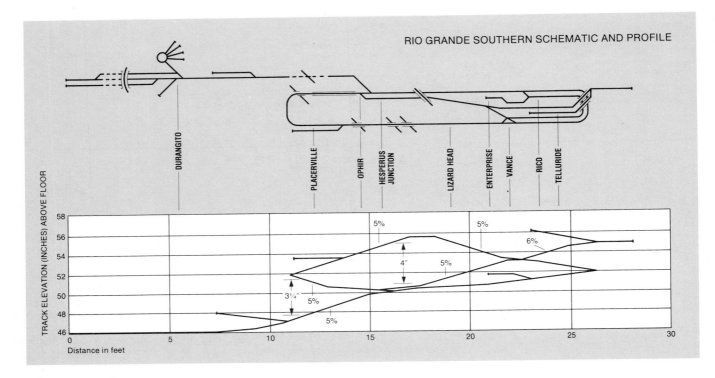

TRACK ELEVATION (INCHES) ABOVE FLOOR

DURANGITO

PLACERVILLE

OPHIR

HESPERUS JUNCTION

LIZARD HEAD

ENTERPRISE

VANCE

RICO

TELLURIDE

5%

5%

6%

4"

5%

3¼"

5%

5%

Distance in feet

room size is equal to about 3½ x 4½ squares. A "waterwings" main line is about all that will fit, but that achieves a major goal: a walk-in railroad, rather than a doughnut-with-duckunder affair. Over the years, the person-feet of accumulated bending over that will be avoided will be monumental!

The sit-in alcove. The aisle in this layout — it's really more of an alcove — won't be up to normal minimum standards (24" to 30") so the RGS has evolved as more of a sit-in design. The layout height shown is based on a pleasant eye-level view when operating from a seated position in the alcove, with the scenery and upper levels of track towering above in true San Juan country fashion. Stand up, and access to most trackage is fair to good so far as operation is concerned (although a cou-

ple of non-prototypical switch machines at Ophir and Hesperus Junction will be preferable to the hand-throws that are the first choice at foreground points). The backdrop will have to go up before the railroad is filled in, though.

What about subsequent minor maintenance, such as touching up scraped rock should something derail? Because the viewing angle is severely restricted, the back faces of most of the mountains can be left open for easy, if moderately uncomfortable, access from below.

An out-and-back schematic. The schematic is the one which is almost always the best possible for any pike built in an area of about 15 squares where you want any mainline running at all: out-and-back, from a stub terminal to a continuous-run oval with single reversing connection. Tracks in the

stub yard can be longer than those in any yard directly on a continuous-run route, and the stub provides one point which must be operated as a terminal with all the switching that implies.

The necessarily short main line can be traversed as many times as desired before peeling off to the yard to again go through the required stub-terminal moves. With proper placement of the branchline junction switch relative to the reversing connection at least two trips around most of the main line must intervene between the "out" and the "back," ensuring a journey of at least moderately respectable length.

How close to the prototype can we get? Literal interpretation of any extended segment of the trackage or operating pattern of the real RGS is out of the question in this modest area, so the station names copied or adapted can provide only the flavor of its operation.

On the other hand, there is room for individual buildings and structures of only moderately compressed scale, and the rugged terrain used to separate the scenes is thoroughly appropriate. Note that the watercourse emerging unseen behind the Durangito enginehouse flows away from the observer while dropping rapidly (the reverse of the situation with about 99 percent of the streams seen on model railroads). This allows the Ophir trestle to soar almost a hundred scale feet above its gulch without looking unnecessary.

On the backdrop there's nothing to stop us from using a direct copy of the real scene, so we can have famed Lizard Head itself (perhaps even partly in 3-D!) on the distant horizon without having to cover up any of our precious track with snowsheds (as the RGS did).

Otto Perry

Tucked onto rock ledges and towering trestles, the Rio Grande Southern offered a perfect prototype for a model railroad which must make the most of the vertical dimension.

52

The Penn Central (Southern Tier Division)

This plan for a large HO layout features construction in two stages

THERE'S A LOT of rugged scenery and still some rugged, busy railroading in the Allegheny Plateau country of northwestern Pennsylvania and the neighboring sections of western New York (called the "Southern Tier" of counties along the state line). This track plan takes advantage of the monumental, if ill-fated, merger of Pennsy and New York Central to combine features of their lines in this area into a showcase for diesel-era mountain railroading.

Terrain, traffic, trackage, and resulting train movements are generally patterned on the former PRR Williamsport-Buffalo route over Keating Summit and the important but relatively little-known ex-NYC Pennsylvania Di-

vision, which extended south into the coal country by way of Pine Creek and the "Grand Canyon of the East" west of Wellsboro, Pennsylvania.

Lots of diesels; few passengers. As an all-diesel pike, this Penn Central need not concern itself with getting long-cab-overhang 2-10-4s comfortably around curves, and passenger traffic is at a low ebb, with only a vestige of the *Buffalo Day Express* still in scheduled operation with a P-70 coach trailing a few head-end cars. The resulting 26" mainline minimum radius in a large, somewhat irregular T-shaped basement allows planning a long main line with full walk-in aisleways alongside and no visible parallel trackage that shouldn't be there.

Traffic patterns. In accordance with the late-1960s traffic pattern, solid coal trains can move north (with a push over the 2.8 percent climb through Fletcher's Plains). The loaded trains meet their empty counterparts which are likewise circulating over a continuous-run dogbone route provided by an unobtrusive through-the-backdrop connection between West End and Lakemont Junction. Merchandise and miscellaneous traffic in closed-top cars (whose loaded or empty state is less apparent) generally move loop-to-loop, covering the entire three-scale-mile main line.

Superimposed on the through traffic is heavy tonnage from on-line sources, including a counterflow of coal from a

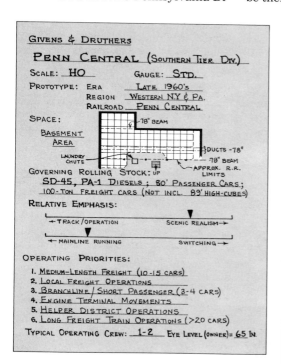

GIVENS & DRUTHERS

PENN CENTRAL (SOUTHERN TIER DIV.)

SCALE: **HO**   GAUGE: **STD.**

PROTOTYPE: ERA   LATE 1960's
        REGION   WESTERN NY & PA.
        RAILROAD   PENN CENTRAL

SPACE:

BASEMENT AREA

GOVERNING ROLLING STOCK: up
SD-45, PA-1 DIESELS; 80' PASSENGER CARS;
100-TON FREIGHT CARS (NOT INCL. 89' HIGH-CUBES)

RELATIVE EMPHASIS:

← TRACK/OPERATION   SCENIC REALISM →

← MAINLINE RUNNING   SWITCHING →

OPERATING PRIORITIES:
1. MEDIUM-LENGTH FREIGHT (10-15 CARS)
2. LOCAL FREIGHT OPERATIONS
3. BRANCHLINE/SHORT PASSENGER (3-4 CARS)
4. ENGINE TERMINAL MOVEMENTS
5. HELPER DISTRICT OPERATIONS
6. LONG FREIGHT TRAIN OPERATIONS (>20 CARS)

TYPICAL OPERATING CREW: **1-2**   EYE LEVEL (OWNER)= **65** IN.

Scenery drawn from the rugged mountains of Pennsylvania and the Southern Tier counties of New York will form the background for this large Penn Central HO layout. True to its prototype and era, much of the equipment will carry NYC (top right, at Marsh Creek, Pa.) or PRR (right, at Sunbury, Pa.) markings instead of the post-merger PC colors.

David R. Connor

Don Wood

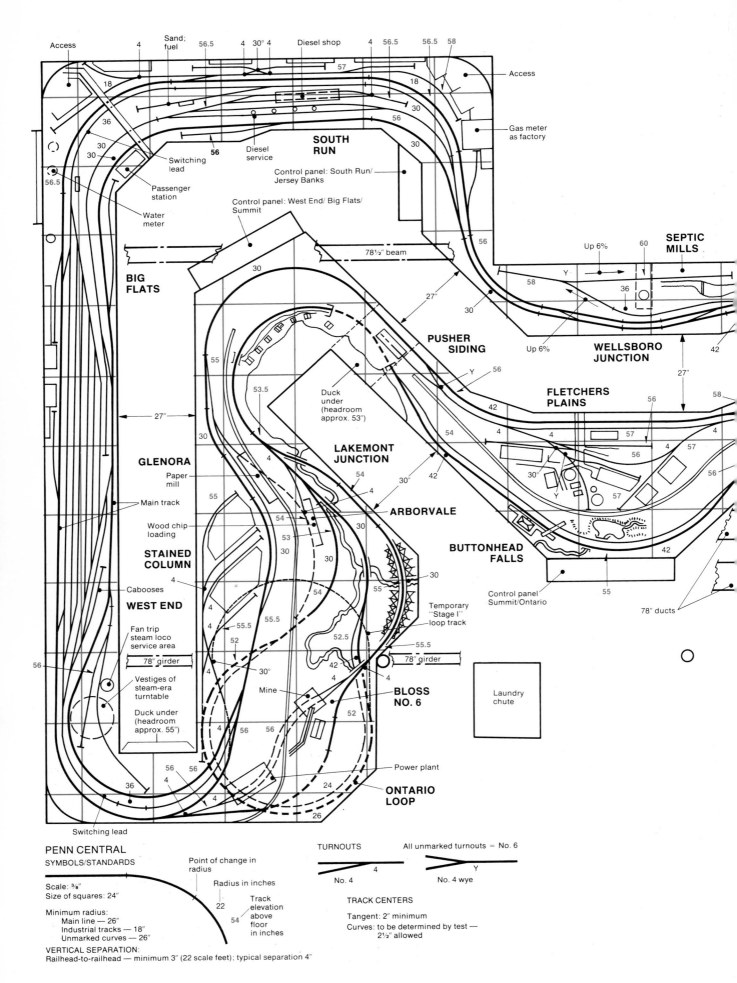

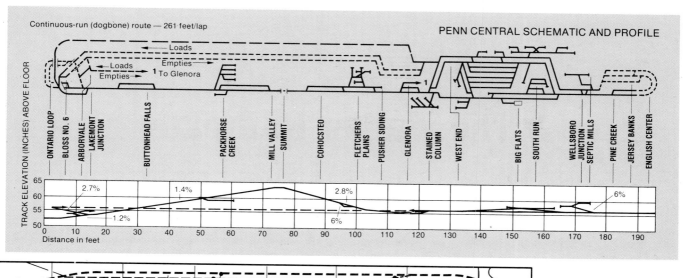

Continuous-run (dogbone) route — 261 feet/lap

Loads

Loads
Empties
Empties → 1 To Glenora

TRACK ELEVATION (INCHES) ABOVE FLOOR

ONTARIO LOOP | BLOSS NO. 6 | ARBORVALE | LAKEMONT JUNCTION | BUTTONHEAD FALLS | PACKHORSE CREEK | MILL VALLEY SUMMIT | COHOCSTEO | FLETCHERS PLAINS | PUSHER SIDING | GLENORA | STAINED COLUMN | WEST END | BIG FLATS | SOUTH RUN | WELLSBORO JUNCTION | SEPTIC MILLS | PINE CREEK | JERSEY BANKS | ENGLISH CENTER

2.7%   1.4%   2.8%   6%
1.2%   6%

Distance in feet

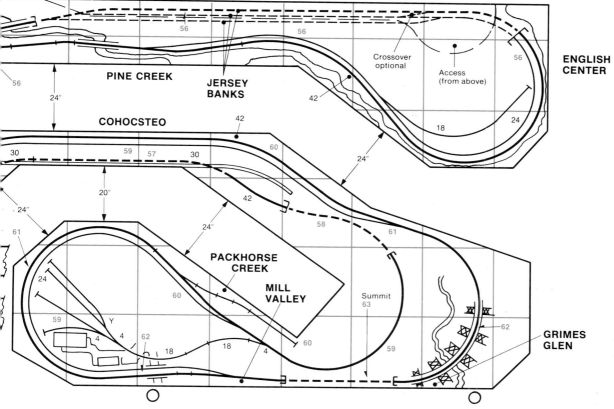

PINE CREEK — JERSEY BANKS — COHOCSTEO — PACKHORSE CREEK — MILL VALLEY

Crossover optional — Access (from above) — ENGLISH CENTER

Summit 63 — GRIMES GLEN

recently reopened north-end mine (Bloss No. 6) to a power plant at West End. Forest products are also making a comeback; this country was the timber capital of the world when first logged off around the turn of the century, and now its second- and third-growth trees feed paper mills again in multi-car shipments. Fletcher's Plains, Mill Valley, and Wellsboro Junction have retained some diversified industries that support local freight turns out of Big Flats in more traditional fashion.

South Run is a major diesel service and running-repair point, with a diverse collection of PC, ex-NYC, and ex-PRR units in various paint and non-paint schemes attracting the railfans and keeping the hostlers busy combining the serviceable units into combinations appropriate for the routes and tonnages of trains leaving Big Flats.

At the far end of the yard — which can be worked from both ends when times are busy — are vestiges of the old steam servicing facilities at West End. Should circumstances continue to point toward more steam fan trip operations, the Penn Central's decision to fill in the old turntable pit might be retroactively reversed by the layout owner — the space is still there. Meanwhile, operating any kind of single-ended power involves interesting complications.

Two-stage construction. Any model railroad this big can benefit from being constructed in stages. To provide modest initial operation before the huge peninsula of benchwork from Grimes Glen to the Arborvale area blocks easy and direct access for construction of the along-the-wall English Center-Stained Column section (which will naturally

be built first), a temporary loop track at Stained Column is shown as a logical possibility. Should this continuous operation be so easy and satisfying that self-discipline may be insufficient to ensure the timely continuation of construction, temporary out-and-back running from Big Flats enforced by refraining from making the interim connection may be better psychology. The track plan leaves either course of action available.

In any case, benchwork design for the layout should provide maximum-headroom duckunders at the West End and Pusher Siding locations, and probably at Cohocsteo as well. Walking along with your train and enjoying the sight as it passes all these scenic wonders is the way to go during railroad operations, but it can be an awfully long way to go to pick up a screwdriver.

The Walker Railroad

This point-to-point On3 railroad incorporates extra space for scenery, as well as intriguing mine diorama and lighting ideas

ALL MODEL RAILROADS are compromises with reality — in any scale, the prototype is just too long and too narrow for direct representation in any practical space. Furthermore, as our live-steam, outdoor compatriots know, the question of where the full-scale trainwatcher stands (or crouches) to watch the small-scale trains always has to be resolved, usually in some

manner that requires a grossly disproportionate footage of trestlework. The On3 Walker Railroad, however, minimizes compromise, to a rare and perhaps even unique degree.

A modest railroad for an immodest space. First, a modest amount of railroad is to be planned for a far larger than average space — a railroad-only basement designed and built for that purpose, with truss joists allowing a column-free room 39' x 56'. The clear ceiling height is more than 9', freeing mainline profiles (and aisleway floor heights) to include long grades without coming too close to the overhead. A spiral-staircase entry near the middle of the room saves even more space.

Second, extra depth is to be allowed throughout the plan to accommodate backlighting, keep track away from background scenery, and generally enhance the feeling of little trains lost in the immensity of the mountains and desert expanses typical of eastern California and neighboring Nevada.

Third, as an On3 pike, the Walker Railroad already has the advantages of ¼" scale in inherent realism that come from the closer-to-reality viewing distances, weight, and sound. Half-inch scale would be still better, of course, but we do have to stop somewhere.

To go with the "total realism" concept which calls for strictly point-to-point operation free from such fakery

as return loops (at least, on the basic narrow gauge Walker Railroad), rolling stock will be limited to that necessary for a railroad providing transportation of the type and quantity needed by the industries and population appropriate for the territory.

Completely specific; utterly plausible. The locale is completely specific — the Walker is a railroad running from Bodie, California, to a connection with the standard gauge Virginia & Truckee at Minden, Nevada, via the most practical route. The scenario is also highly developed so as to be both plausible and without too much direct conflict between what did happen and what might have happened in the area. The Walker Railroad is a successor to the very real (and rather well documented) 3' gauge Bodie & Benton, which hauled mine timbers and not much else into Bodie from the south from 1881 to 1917.

The Walker, supposedly built from Bodie northward in the early 1920s, took over some of the B & B's moldering rolling stock, added other hand-me-downs, and is serving its mining, oil, ranching, and timber customers in moderately prosperous fashion in the 1939 era represented in the model. In the real world these traffic sources didn't materialize, of course — perhaps only because of lack of an entrepreneurial type like the model railroader who has conceived and is building the

GIVENS & DRUTHERS

WALKER R R and VIRGINIA & TRUCKEE connection

SCALE: O   GAUGE: n3/STD.

PROTOTYPE: ERA 1939
            REGION CALIFORNIA - NEVADA
            RAILROAD Bodie & Benton / Va. & Truckee

SPACE: 110" CLEAR
                                    CEILING
BASEMENT 39'   PREFABRICATED
NO COLUMNS,   SPIRAL STAIRCASE
NO UTILITIES   (48" O.D.)
            56'

GOVERNING ROLLING STOCK:
NARROW GAUGE: K-27 2-8-2, 40' PSGR. CARS
STANDARD GAUGE: V&T 4-6-0, 65' PSGR. CARS

RELATIVE EMPHASIS:
←TRACK/OPERATION   SCENIC REALISM→
←MAINLINE RUNNING   SWITCHING→

OPERATING PRIORITIES:
1. BRANCH/LOCAL PSGR. & MIXED
2. LOCAL FREIGHT
3. MEDIUM-LENGTH FREIGHT (10-15 CARS)
4. HELPER DISTRICT OPERATIONS
5. TIMETABLE OPERATION (FAST CLOCK)
6.

TYPICAL OPERATING CREW: 1-2 EYE LEVEL (OWNER) = 62 IN.

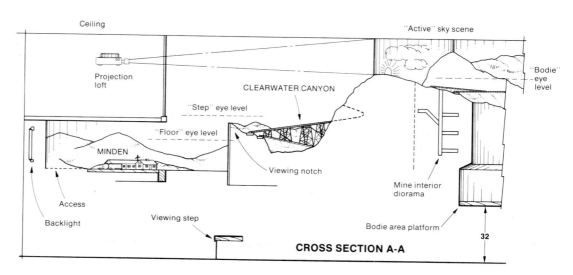

Ceiling

Projection loft

"Active" sky scene

CLEARWATER CANYON

"Bodie" eye level

"Step" eye level

"Floor" eye level

Viewing notch

MINDEN

Mine interior diorama

Access

Backlight

Viewing step

Bodie area platform

32

CROSS SECTION A-A

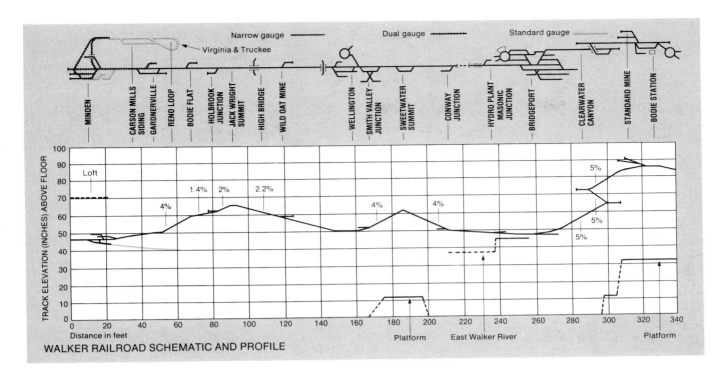

NARROW GAUGE ← | → DUAL GAUGE ← | → STANDARD GAUGE

Virginia & Truckee

MINDEN — CARSON MILLS SIDING — GARDNERVILLE — RENO LOOP — BODIE FLAT — HOLBROOK JUNCTION — JACK WRIGHT SUMMIT — HIGH BRIDGE — WILD OAT MINE — WELLINGTON — SMITH VALLEY JUNCTION — SWEETWATER SUMMIT — CONWAY JUNCTION — HYDRO PLANT — MASONIC JUNCTION — BRIDGEPORT — CLEARWATER CANYON — STANDARD MINE — BODIE STATION

WALKER RAILROAD SCHEMATIC AND PROFILE

basement and its contents — but it very well could have, and the mountains, watercourses, and plains depicted on today's topographical maps are still the shape they were then.

Using these maps, it's no problem to pick out almost exactly the route that full-scale civil engineers would have selected to join the two terminals. The resulting railroad would be 85.5 miles long, descending from an almost-alpine 8500' elevation at Bodie to 4725' at Minden via two major intermediate summits. The line would involve three to four percent grades unless financially ridiculous grading and tunneling were used to achieve a trunk-line alignment.

A relaxed track plan. The resulting track plan, with the relaxation that a space equivalent to 8½ x 13 squares allows, is of the standard walk-in pattern that we'd always like to have — only more so. Not only can you follow the

main line continuously over its scale 3.3 miles (which means that it is 1/25 as long as the real thing, a far better ratio than typical in modeling any railroad which is much more than a mere shortline spur) but there are plenty of wide spots in the aisles for better viewing or photography.

At various points the integrity of along-the-track views is enhanced by aisle-side view-blocks extending above eye level. These help keep extraneous items — such as an unrelated section of the main line across the aisle — from intruding on the scene. For a direct view at these points there are permanent steps available for a convenient peek. At two points (between Jack Wright Summit and Holbrook and in Phantom Canyon on the way up to Sweetwater Summit) the scenery can properly extend far below the tracks, perhaps all the way to the floor.

The major ups and downs of the

aisleways to match eye and track levels have side benefits — shop and material storage areas can underlap the railroad. No matter how liberal the area available, making the best use of it is still well worthwhile.

Relaxed operation, too. The railroad itself is relatively simple, with only those turnouts or other complications strictly necessary to handle an assumed moderate but diversified traffic level. Passing tracks are short because the chance of two long trains meeting is small, if only because the line simply doesn't have that much rolling stock.

Loaded traffic toward Minden picks up considerably at Smith Valley Junction and Wellington, so the surveyors picked out a "Georgetown Loop" alignment to reduce the grade to about half that over Sweetwater Summit (and half the grade which must be surmounted when southbound with the empties). Thus the same motive power

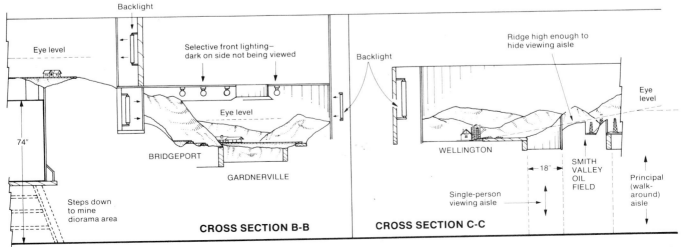

CROSS SECTION B-B

CROSS SECTION C-C

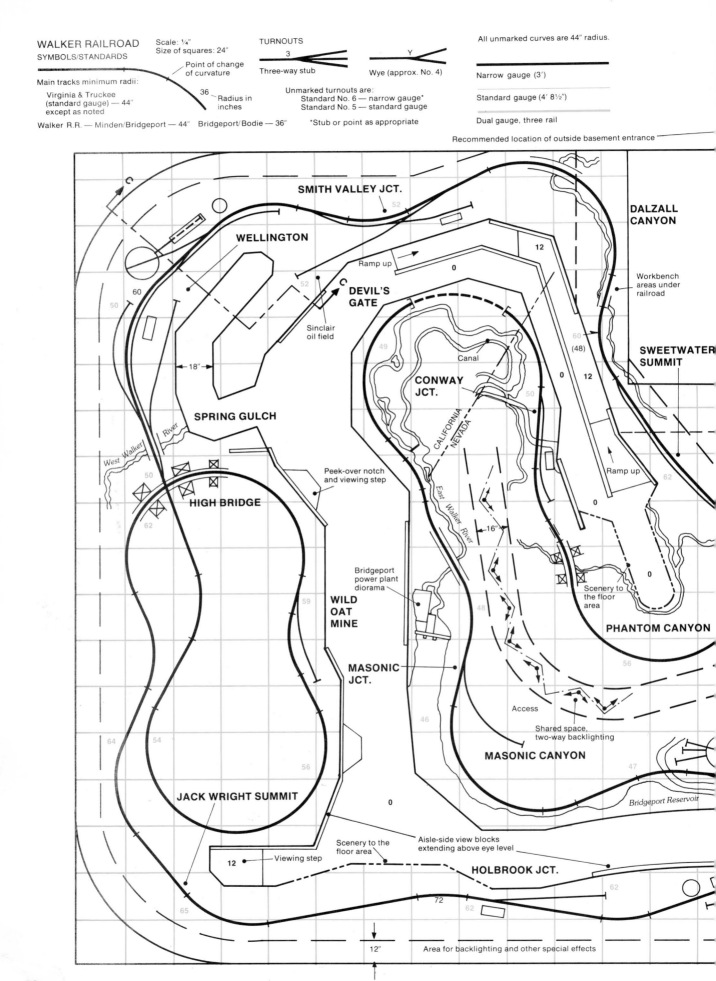

WALKER RAILROAD
SYMBOLS/STANDARDS

Scale: ¼"
Size of squares: 24"

Main tracks minimum radii:

Virginia & Truckee
(standard gauge) — 44"
except as noted

Walker R.R. — Minden/Bridgeport — 44"   Bridgeport/Bodie — 36"

Point of change
of curvature

36 Radius in
inches

TURNOUTS

3
Three-way stub

Y
Wye (approx. No. 4)

Unmarked turnouts are:
Standard No. 6 — narrow gauge*
Standard No. 5 — standard gauge

*Stub or point as appropriate

All unmarked curves are 44" radius.

Narrow gauge (3')

Standard gauge (4' 8½")

Dual gauge, three rail

Recommended location of outside basement entrance

SMITH VALLEY JCT.   52

DALZALL
CANYON

WELLINGTON

DEVIL'S
GATE

Sinclair
oil field

Ramp up

12

0

Workbench
areas under
railroad

60
50

18"

SPRING GULCH

West Walker River

50

62

HIGH BRIDGE

49

CONWAY
JCT.

Canal

CALIFORNIA
NEVADA

50

60
(48)

0   12

SWEETWATER
SUMMIT

Ramp up

62

0

Peek-over notch
and viewing step

East Walker River

16"

Bridgeport power plant
diorama

WILD
OAT
MINE

59

MASONIC
JCT.

48

Scenery to
the floor
area

PHANTOM CANYON

56

64   54

56

46

JACK WRIGHT SUMMIT

0

Access

Shared space,
two-way backlighting

MASONIC CANYON

47

Bridgeport Reservoir

12   Viewing step

Scenery to the
floor area

Aisle-side view blocks
extending above eye level

HOLBROOK JCT.

62

65   72   62

12"   Area for backlighting and other special effects

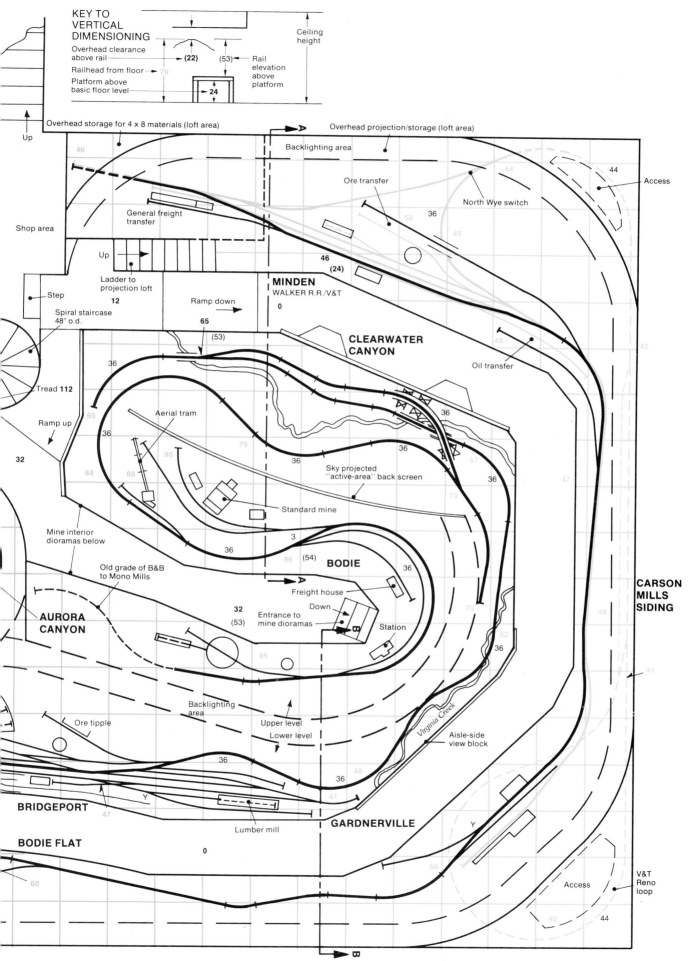

KEY TO VERTICAL DIMENSIONING
Overhead clearance above rail → (22)
Railhead from floor → 79
Platform above basic floor level → 24
Ceiling height
(53) → Rail elevation above platform

Overhead storage for 4 x 8 materials (loft area)
Overhead projection/storage (loft area)
Backlighting area
46
Ore transfer
44
44
Access
North Wye switch
Shop area
General freight transfer
50
36
45
Up
46
(24)
48
Ladder to projection loft
Up
MINDEN
WALKER R.R./V&T
0
Step
12
Ramp down
Oil transfer
Spiral staircase 48" o.d.
CLEARWATER CANYON
65
(53)
42
Tread 112
36
36
Ramp up
65
48
Aerial tram
36
57
32
90
36
47
84
88
Sky projected "active-area" back screen
73
Standard mine
Mine interior dioramas below
3
86
(54)
BODIE
36
Old grade of B&B to Mono Mills
36
73
48
AURORA CANYON
32
(53)
Entrance to mine dioramas
Freight house
Down
Station
52
36
85
41
CARSON MILLS SIDING
Backlighting area
Upper level
Lower level
Ore tipple
Virginia Creek
Aisle-side view block
36
36
48
BRIDGEPORT
47
Y
47
Lumber mill
GARDNERVILLE
Y
BODIE FLAT
0
50
60
Access
V&T Reno loop
40
44
B

Inspiration for the Walker Railroad comes chiefly from the Bodie & Benton, a narrow gauge line that was abandoned in 1917. The Walker's standard gauge interchange is with the Virginia & Truckee (above), a Nevada gold-hauler. The V & T did in fact in-terchange with a three foot gauge road, the Carson & Colorado, which later became the Keeler Branch of the Southern Pacific (above right). (Below) The Walker will also borrow scenery from spectacular Phantom Canyon on the D & RGW narrow gauge.

William Botkin

can cope with the longer consists when headed for Jack Wright Summit. In any case, many train miles on the Walker will be with helper locos attached.

Bodie gives the impression of being high up because it is high — it is reached only via a double switchback with geared-loco grades in a separate operation out of the main operating hub at Bridgeport.

Special effects. The proprietor is also interested in mining technology typical of the era and locale, so there is ample room for subterranean modeling of the gold ore extraction process, with step-down access to stand-up viewing. How do you model these shafts, stopes, and adits so you can see what's going on and still have the feel of being underground? That's one of the things he

expects to work out during the projected 10 to 20 years of construction before the "railroad" is reasonably complete.

Also requiring development is the "active" sky over Bodie, which will be backlit by a projector. It should be possible to have real-time thunderstorms as well as sunrises and other calmer progressions from one weather or lighting condition to another. Will it be worthwhile? That can't be guaranteed, but the space and facilities for doing it have been provided.

The standard gauge connection. The connecting V & T is represented by an out-and-back operation from Minden to a concealed loop and staging siding, with only the amount of dual-gauge trackage that would be likely in such an end-to-end connection. The

third-rail extension of the V & T over the Walker is based on the projected-but-never-built Gardnerville & Northern, which stemmed from a rivalry between the "twin cities" of Gardnerville and Minden and their respective businessmen. The V & T handles only passenger and express traffic on its back-in/pull-out trips to serve its alternate southern terminal; freight interchange is at Minden, in three different modes for welcome variety.

Scenic considerations. Scenery is to be copied almost directly from the real thing in most cases. Phantom Canyon, however, has been borrowed from its namesake Phantom Curve on the Antonito-Durango line of the D & RGW, where weird rock formations cause shadows from the headlight of an approaching locomotive to appear to race across the canyon walls — something just too good to leave out, and also something that will no doubt require some experimentation to pull off convincingly.

At various points the relaxed, spacious design might seem to result in scenes too deep for satisfactory access to track in the background. As illustrated in cross section C-C at Wellington, hidden access can be provided if it's properly considered in working out the terrain contours.

As a final touch in the quest for total-immersion effects on visitors the normal entry to the railroad is via about one and a quarter turns of a spiral staircase, which should prove thoroughly disorienting. The outside entrance to the shop area is essential for getting 4' x 8' sheets of building materials into the construction scene, and since the railroad is to be built in Alaska, sufficient storage for a long winter's work is highly desirable if a snow shovel isn't to be a major energy-consumer on the project.

The Great Northern Railway and Montana & Golden Gate Railroad

Two mainline railroads through the mountains, steam and electrified, with a branch to Glacier Park

THIS EXPANSIVE HO version of the Great Northern is to share the ground floor of a typical San Francisco townhouse with a second hobby (gardening), an automobile, and the more typical basement impedimenta such as a furnace, water heater, and laundry. Unlike most basement garages, this one was built when this city's rules did not require that it be walled off from other areas on the same floor; with the locational freedom this gives a model railroad goes the agony of decisions. Are we sure that cars will continue to get more compact for the life of the railroad? Coming down a precipitous street and making a right-angle turn into the garage is a bit hairy at best — how accurately can we count on positioning the vehicle, *every time*? Everything that goes to or from the garden has to pass through the railroad area — how compatible is HO gauge with topsoil and fertilizer?

Well, with a certain amount of faith, here's the plan for the Great Northern and its connecting line, the electrified Montana & Golden Gate, which parallels and then crosses the Big G on its diagonal way to California. The M & GG would be the Milwaukee Road except that the operational concept for this layout calls for lots of passenger switching and interchange, and that makes more sense if the electrified road has a less directly competitive destination.

The specifications. The basic objective of this model railroad is to re-create the sight of the *Empire Builder* and its kin in their late-1940s livery rolling through spacious Big Sky scenes and railroad towns over spectacular but not steeply graded sections of railroad. The proprietor has no desire to represent helper-district operations, nor is he willing to sacrifice scenic grandeur to the space required for an engine terminal.

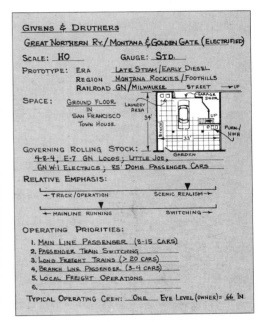

GIVENS & DRUTHERS

GREAT NORTHERN RY./ MONTANA & GOLDEN GATE (ELECTRIFIED)

SCALE: HO   GAUGE: STD.

PROTOTYPE: ERA   LATE STEAM / EARLY DIESEL
           REGION   MONTANA ROCKIES / FOOTHILLS
           RAILROAD   GN / MILWAUKEE

SPACE: GROUND FLOOR IN SAN FRANCISCO TOWN HOUSE

GOVERNING ROLLING STOCK: 4-8-4, E-7 GN LOCOS; LITTLE JOE, GN W-1 ELECTRICS; 85' DOME PASSENGER CARS

RELATIVE EMPHASIS:

← TRACK / OPERATION   SCENIC REALISM →

← MAINLINE RUNNING   SWITCHING →

OPERATING PRIORITIES:
1. MAIN LINE PASSENGER (8-15 CARS)
2. PASSENGER TRAIN SWITCHING
3. LONG FREIGHT TRAINS (> 20 CARS)
4. BRANCH LINE PASSENGER (3-4 CARS)
5. LOCAL FREIGHT OPERATIONS
6.

TYPICAL OPERATING CREW: ONE   EYE LEVEL (OWNER) = 66 IN.

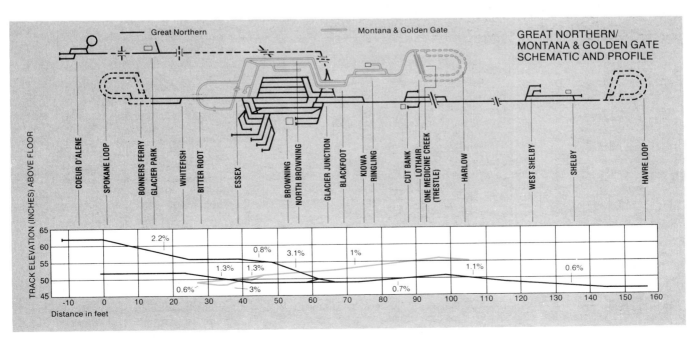

GREAT NORTHERN/ MONTANA & GOLDEN GATE SCHEMATIC AND PROFILE

Great Northern ——   Montana & Golden Gate

COEUR D'ALENE · SPOKANE LOOP · BONNERS FERRY · GLACIER PARK · WHITEFISH · BITTER ROOT · ESSEX · BROWNING · NORTH BROWNING · GLACIER JUNCTION · BLACKFOOT · KIOWA · RINGLING · CUT BANK · LOTHAIR · ONE MEDICINE CREEK (TRESTLE) · HARLOW · WEST SHELBY · SHELBY · HAVRE LOOP

TRACK ELEVATION (INCHES) ABOVE FLOOR

2.2%   0.8%   3.1%   1%   1.1%   0.6%
1.3%   1.3%
0.6%   3%   0.7%

Distance in feet

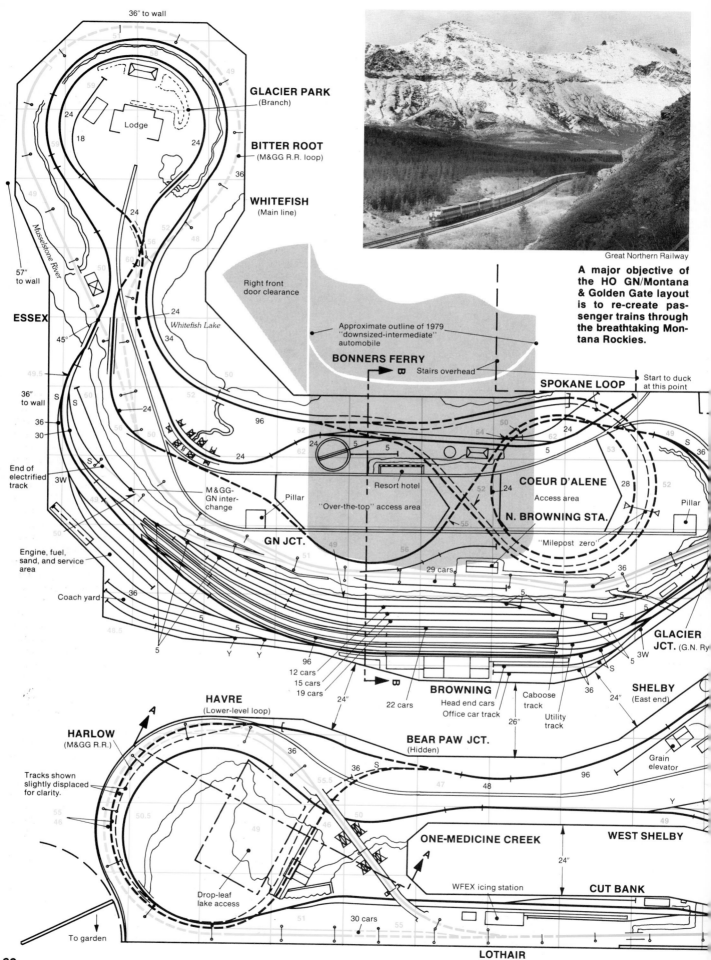

36" to wall

51
58
49

GLACIER PARK
(Branch)

59

24

Lodge

18   24

BITTER ROOT
(M&GG R.R. loop)

36

52
56
48

WHITEFISH
(Main line)

Musselstone River

57"
to wall

49

50
60

Right front
door clearance

ESSEX

45°

24

Whitefish Lake

34

Approximate outline of 1979
"downsized-intermediate"
automobile

96

SPOKANE LOOP

Start to duck
at this point

49.5

52

52

50

BONNERS FERRY   Stairs overhead

50
54

24

49   S

36

36"
to wall

36
30

24

50

62

24   5   5

52

COEUR D'ALENE

53

28   52

Resort hotel

Access area

End of
electrified
track

3W

S   S

49

M&GG-
GN inter-
change

Pillar

"Over-the-top" access area

55

N. BROWNING STA.

"Milepost zero"

Pillar

50

GN JCT.

51   49   56

29 cars

36

Engine, fuel,
sand, and service
area

5

GLACIER
JCT. (G.N. Ry

Coach yard

36

5   5

5

3W   5   S

36

48.5

5

Y   Y

96

12 cars
15 cars
19 cars

24"

22 cars

BROWNING

Head end cars
Office car track

Caboose
track

Utility
track

26"

SHELBY
(East end)

24"

HAVRE
(Lower-level loop)

A

BEAR PAW JCT.
(Hidden)

36

Grain
elevator

HARLOW
(M&GG R.R.)

Tracks shown
slightly displaced
for clarity.

55

36   S

55.5

47   48

96

Y

49

55
46

50.5

50

46

WEST SHELBY

One-MEDICINE CREEK

49

24"

Drop-leaf
lake access

A

WFEX icing station

CUT BANK

To garden

51

30 cars

55

LOTHAIR

Great Northern Railway

**A major objective of
the HO GN/Montana
& Golden Gate layout
is to re-create pas-
senger trains through
the breathtaking Mon-
tana Rockies.**

GREAT NORTHERN/MONTANA & GOLDEN GATE

SYMBOLS/STANDARDS

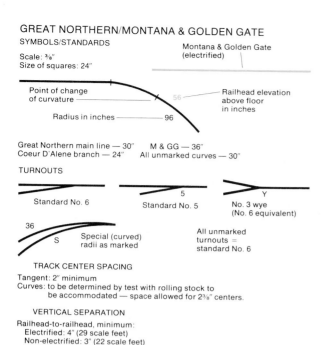

Scale: ⅜"
Size of squares: 24"

Montana & Golden Gate
(electrified)

Point of change
of curvature

Radius in inches ——— 96

56 —— Railhead elevation
above floor
in inches

Great Northern main line — 30"
Coeur D'Alene branch — 24"

M & GG — 36"
All unmarked curves — 30"

TURNOUTS

Standard No. 6

5
Standard No. 5

Y
No. 3 wye
(No. 6 equivalent)

36
S
Special (curved)
radii as marked

All unmarked
turnouts =
standard No. 6

TRACK CENTER SPACING

Tangent: 2" minimum
Curves: to be determined by test with rolling stock to
be accommodated — space allowed for 2⅜" centers.

VERTICAL SEPARATION

Railhead-to-railhead, minimum:
Electrified: 4" (29 scale feet)
Non-electrified: 3" (22 scale feet)

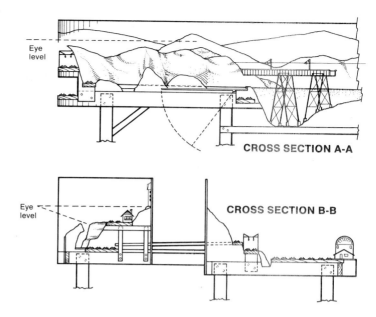

Eye
level

CROSS SECTION A-A

Eye
level

CROSS SECTION B-B

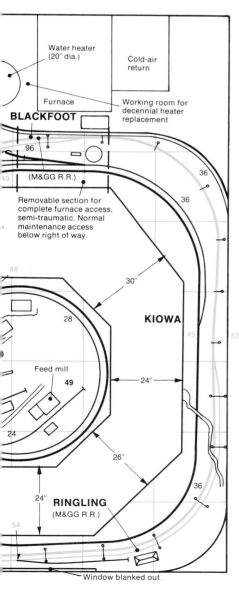

Water heater
(20" dia.)

Cold-air
return

Furnace

Working room for
decennial heater
replacement

BLACKFOOT

96

(M&GG R.R.)

Removable section for
complete furnace access,
semi-traumatic. Normal
maintenance access
below right of way.

48

30"

28

KIOWA

Feed mill
49

24"

24

26"

24"
RINGLING
(M&GG R.R.)

54

Window blanked out.

49

49

53

36

36

36

In line with these specifications, and taking full advantage of the stipulation that the automobile will be parked elsewhere during serious railroad operation, this Great Northern pretty well fills its 27′ x 28′ area in wrapping a loop-to-loop main line alongside meandering, walk-in aisles. As cross section B-B shows, some of the most scenic and complex trackwork is over the hood of the car when the garage is so occupied, but reasonable clearance has been included to ensure that a sudden clutch engagement in reverse won't cause substantial hood damage — plus instant elevation of Bonners Ferry and Coeur d'Alene.

A centerpiece and an omission. The centerpiece of the railroad is the extensive division point at Browning. Primarily passenger-train oriented, it has facilities for servicing two lengthy limiteds at once as well as handling connecting trains to and from the Coeur d'Alene branch. In conveying through Pullman passengers to the resort hotels at its terminal station the branch also brings them practically to the front steps of Glacier Park Lodge.

A notable omission at Browning is the typical division-point roundhouse. A pioneer in extended engine runs with its oilburners, the Big G has been sending its 4-8-4s through here without engine change or servicing for so long that the only motive power facilities are some open tracks and a one-stall house sufficient to take care of switchers and the branch local's engine. On the other hand, the up-front coach yards are usually filled with extra sleepers, diners, and coaches supporting the resort traffic. The wye leading

to the sharply curved branch maintains the 30″ minimum radius — standard for the GN main line — far enough beyond its third switch to allow any class of locomotive to use it for turning.

Accommodating the electrics. The big electrics on the Montana & Golden Gate (Little Joes, and those 100′-long GN W-1 B-D + D-Bs) rate a 36″ minimum radius on its main tracks. Maintaining the proper relative position for a catenary-equipped line on any model railroad (at the rear wherever possible, so that a careless hand won't snag the wire while tinkering with or pointing at something in the foreground), the M & GG manages to parallel the GN for more than a scale mile between partially concealed end loops. An inconvenient connecting track across the Musselstone River makes for interesting switching in exchanging through passenger cars between the two roads' limiteds.

Station names on both lines are generally in correct east-west sequence and were selected to convey the feeling of the Montana-Idaho territory of the prototypes, but they attempt only limited correlation with the population, trackage, or scenery of their namesakes.

A potentially awkward access situation occurs in the area between Browning and Bonners Ferry, where whole helices of track have to be concealed, the catenary can only be reached from the front over a wide expanse of yard, and the staircase to the house proper intervenes awkwardly. The answer is to leave an 18″ space between backdrops, thus allowing over-the-top access to both sides from a step stool within the opening.

The Durango, Ophir & Northern Railroad

This mountain railroad features a scenic divider in the middle of the main yard so it can serve as both terminals

SUPPOSE FOR A MOMENT that the rail line connecting the Santa Fe, New Mexico, area with Telluride and Ridgway, Colorado, had (like the real-life Colorado Midland) been standard gauge. Suppose, also, that it took a route that passed through Durango, Colorado, and used some of the same passes actually occupied by the Rio Grande Southern and the Denver & Rio Grande narrow gauge lines in approaching the same mining areas. Further suppose that this railroad, once the D & RG had converted its Tennessee Pass main line to standard gauge,

had built a branch over to Glenwood Springs to connect and interchange with its neighbor.

Well, there's your imaginary prototype for the Durango, Ophir & Northern, and by 1900 its compact 4-6-0 and 2-8-0 locomotives are wriggling up, around, over, and through the rugged San Juan country on a busy line that manages to tap all sorts of revenue sources — livestock, coal, people — in addition to handling bridge and interline traffic derived from its several connections.

An ambitious mountain railroad. In

model form this ambitious HO mountain railroad must be fitted into a 17 x 19-foot basement room. Even if we peer into the future a few years beyond the era chosen and envision the addition of early 0-6-6-0 and 2-6-6-2 Mallet "superpower" units to the roster a 22" radius should be adequate for the main line, with the branch — restricted as it is to smaller engines — going down to 18" wherever necessary.

The resulting 8 x 8½ square area will permit a nice walk-in arrangement, but in the interest of more intensive operation the lines are allowed to

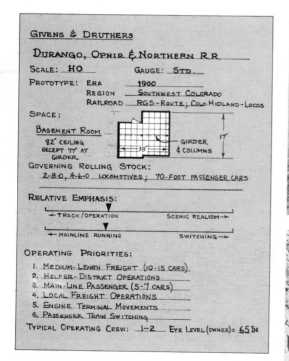

GIVENS & DRUTHERS

DURANGO, OPHIR & NORTHERN R.R.

SCALE: __HO__   GAUGE: __STD.__

PROTOTYPE: ERA   __1900__
            REGION   __SOUTHWEST COLORADO__
            RAILROAD   __RGS - ROUTE; COLO. MIDLAND - LOCOS__

SPACE:

BASEMENT ROOM
82" CEILING
EXCEPT 77" AT
GIRDER   GIRDER
                        & COLUMNS   17'

GOVERNING ROLLING STOCK:
2-8-0, 4-6-0 LOCOMOTIVES; 70-FOOT PASSENGER CARS

RELATIVE EMPHASIS:

← TRACK / OPERATION   SCENIC REALISM →

← MAINLINE RUNNING   SWITCHING →

OPERATING PRIORITIES:
1. MEDIUM-LENGTH FREIGHT (10-15 CARS)
2. HELPER-DISTRICT OPERATIONS
3. MAIN-LINE PASSENGER (5-7 CARS)
4. LOCAL FREIGHT OPERATIONS
5. ENGINE TERMINAL MOVEMENTS
6. PASSENGER TRAIN SWITCHING

TYPICAL OPERATING CREW: __1-2__   EYE LEVEL (OWNER) = __65 IN.__

T. H. Routh: Denver Public Library Western Collection

Based on three railroads — the standard gauge Colorado Midland and the narrow gauge Rio Grande Southern and Denver & Rio Grande — the HO gauge Durango, Ophir & Northern will have plenty of prototype inspiration for its rugged scenery. (Top right) A typical Colorado Midland 4-6-0 with a four-car consist at Glenwood Springs. (Right) A three foot gauge D&RGW train in the Black Canyon with the famed Curecanti Needle rock formation at right. (Far right) A two-car Colorado Midland train on the towering steel bridge near Buena Vista, Colorado, with College Peaks looming behind.

R. H. Kindig

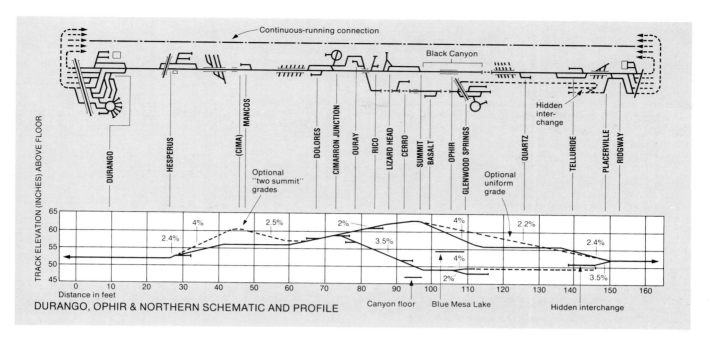

DURANGO, OPHIR & NORTHERN SCHEMATIC AND PROFILE

Continuous-running connection

Black Canyon

Hidden interchange

TRACK ELEVATION (INCHES) ABOVE FLOOR

DURANGO — HESPERUS — (CIMA) MANCOS — DOLORES — CIMARRON JUNCTION — OURAY — RICO — LIZARD HEAD — CERRO — SUMMIT — BASALT — OPHIR — GLENWOOD SPRINGS — QUARTZ — TELLURIDE — PLACERVILLE — RIDGWAY

Optional "two summit" grades

Optional uniform grade

2.4% 4% 2.5% 2% 3.5% 4% 4% 2% 2.2% 2.4% 3.5%

Distance in feet

Canyon floor   Blue Mesa Lake   Hidden interchange

double back on themselves here and there. There are places where the operators will see a train pass by more than once en route from Durango to Glenwood Springs or Ridgway, but amid all those peaks and canyons doubling back wasn't particularly unusual in the prototype — and a main line almost three scale miles long is reckoned to be well worth it.

One yard equals two terminals.

There obviously is room for only a single main yard, and it would be hard put to originate enough trains for the mainline traffic desired, so I have selected a basically continuous-run schematic. The moderately novel wrinkle is locating this through yard where its two end ladders represent the two supposedly distant terminals of the line, Durango and Ridgway. A thoroughly opaque view block over the middle of

the yard tracks does the trick. In theory, as busy and important stops on the line from Santa Fe to Grand Junction, Colorado, the big Durango and Ridgway stations each rate extra passing tracks — which will be used instead as switching leads to work the yards without blocking the flow of mainline traffic in or out.

Principal engine facilities are at Durango, with just a two-stall shed at

W. H. Jackson: Denver Public Library Western Collection

Ridgway serving the helper engines and occasional road engines that terminate their runs there. We could justify having a roundhouse at Ridgway, too, but on this layout one fair-sized roundhouse beats the two little ones that might otherwise be fitted into the same total area, especially when what the proprietor is out to do is capture the look of a busy railroad that has grown beyond shortline status.

What do you do with a locomotive that has pushed a heavy freight from Ridgway up to Lizard Head, turned on the wye, and returned to its base for the next helper assignment, now headed the wrong way? After a quick glance in all directions, you sneak it under the barrier to the Durango turntable and back when nobody's looking! Despite this cheating the layout includes three turntables, which would be too many to maintain if this were a modern or late steam era pike where they would have to be motor-driven. Since these 1900-period tables need no such refinements and manually operated models are both simple and reliable, the Cimarron Junction-to-Glenwood Springs branch can be provided with the facilities for operating assigned power right-end-to at all times.

Generating traffic for the branch. To provide the stiffly graded Glenwood Springs branch with enough connecting D & RG carloads to make it look like a line worth building through such rugged territory there is a two-track hidden D & RG interchange arrangement tucked away under Telluride; its other leg represents yet another connection with the Rio Grande off the main line over near Ridgway. The ends of the interchange tracks below Telluride also serve as an inconspicuous place to "fiddle" rolling stock between the layout and off-track storage when the car supply begins to outstrip the layout's capacity.

A walk-in aisleway up Black Canyon in the center of the layout would be the standard way to make this breathtaking segment of main line accessible and visible, but there just isn't room for one. Also, the highly desirable branch line across the mouth of the canyon would block the walk-in access. The answer offered here is to provide access for when something goes wrong via the drop-down surface of Blue Mesa Lake, thereby allowing the scenic treatment to provide an unusual lengthwise view up the deep, spectacular gorge to the

distant trestle crossing the headwaters of the lake.

All sorts of optional grades. In profile this track plan has options which can shift train operations toward or away from either short trains or extensive, mandatory use of helper engines. If the grade (as shown in solid line on the profile) is kept relatively constant between Hesperus and Dolores we have asymmetrical grades on the continuous-run main line: Running counterclockwise on the schematic the ruling grade is about 2.4 percent, which should allow many trains to make it without assistance; clockwise, there is a 4 percent pitch in Black Canyon which will usually call for a helper or two. This means you have a choice between two operating patterns: Run 'em one way if you don't want the complication of extra motive power, the other when the fun of helper service fits the mood of the crew.

If more challenging operation at all times is acceptable, a second summit at Mancos will raise the ruling grade to 4 percent in both directions, improve scenic separation between adjacent parallel tracks, and make the overall grade arrangement resemble somewhat more closely the situation on the real Rio Grande Southern in this area, where it was always going either up or down at a dizzying rate.

Yet a third choice, for a relatively easier situation in both directions, is to even out the grade between Placerville and Summit to about 2.2 percent. Well-loaded trains will still look okay with helpers, considering the limited tractive force of the biggest power available in 1900. Take your choice!

A two-stage construction option. With all that track and all those grades the DO & N won't be the quickest model railroad in the world to build, so yet a further option not affecting the completed mainline alignment is two-stage construction. To exercise this option a temporary connection is added above the center of the body tracks in the main Durango/Ridgway yard. This connection allows the around-the-walls portion of the layout to be substantially completed, including building the yard, and considerable mainline operation to take place before building the benchwork in the middle of the room. Since the aisleways in this plan are on the narrow side for accommodating heavy construction, the two-stage option is a possibility well worth considering.

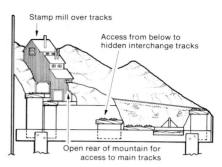

Stamp mill over tracks

Access from below to hidden interchange tracks

Open rear of mountain for access to main tracks

CROSS SECTION A-A

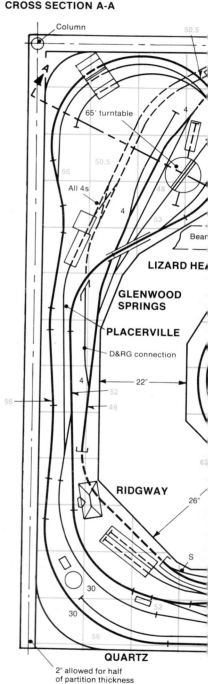

Column

50.5

65' turntable

4

56

50.5

All 4s

48

4

93

Bear

LIZARD HEA

GLENWOOD SPRINGS

PLACERVILLE

D&RG connection

4

22"

56

52

49

RIDGWAY

26"

30

S

30

52

56

QUARTZ

2" allowed for half of partition thickness

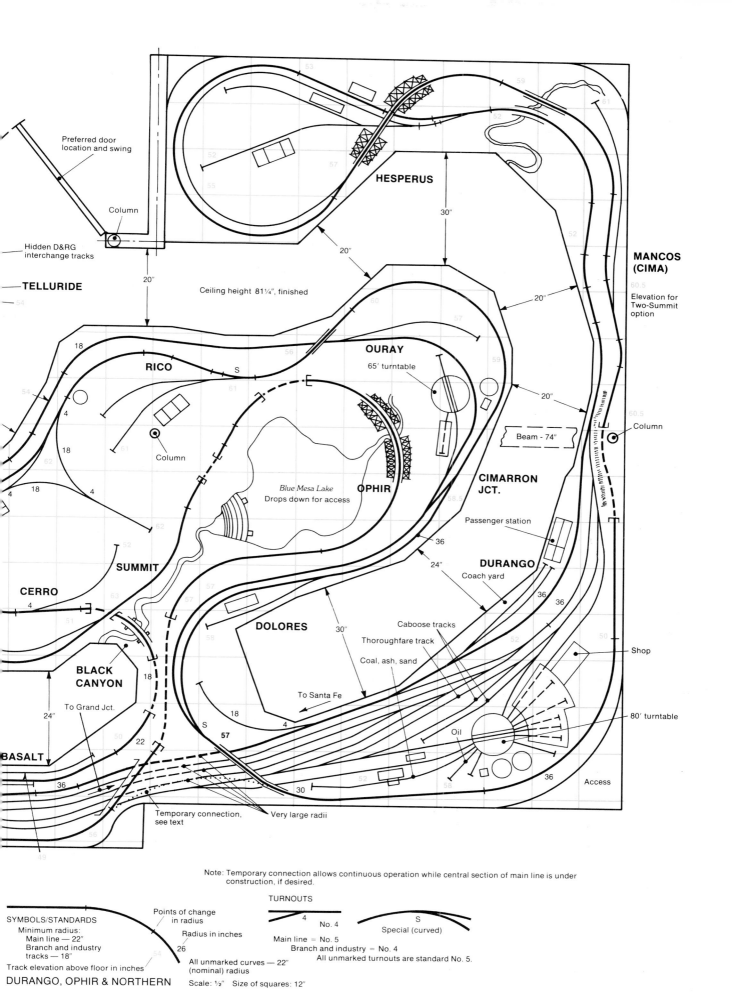

Preferred door
location and swing

Column

Hidden D&RG
interchange tracks

TELLURIDE

— 54

20"

Ceiling height 81¼", finished

HESPERUS

30"

20"

53

52

59

61

57

55

52

**MANCOS
(CIMA)**

60.5

Elevation for
Two-Summit
option

20"

20"

OURAY

65' turntable

60

57

56

S

61

RICO

18

54

4

18

Column

62

18

4

4

18

62

Blue Mesa Lake
Drops down for access

OPHIR

59

20"

60.5

Column

Beam - 74"

**CIMARRON
JCT.**

58.5

Passenger station

DURANGO

Coach yard

36

36

36

24"

52

50

Shop

52

SUMMIT

CERRO

4

63

57

52

Caboose tracks

Thoroughfare track

Coal, ash, sand

30"

DOLORES

51

58

18

**BLACK
CANYON**

18

24"

To Grand Jct.

To Santa Fe

18

4

S

57

80' turntable

Oil

36

Access

BASALT

50

22

36

30

52

58

56

49

Temporary connection,
see text

Very large radii

Note: Temporary connection allows continuous operation while central section of main line is under
construction, if desired.

TURNOUTS

SYMBOLS/STANDARDS
 Minimum radius:
  Main line — 22"
  Branch and industry
  tracks — 18"
Track elevation above floor in inches

Points of change
in radius

Radius in inches

26

54

4   No. 4

S
Special (curved)

Main line = No. 5
 Branch and industry = No. 4
  All unmarked turnouts are standard No. 5.

DURANGO, OPHIR & NORTHERN

All unmarked curves — 22"
(nominal) radius

Scale: ½" Size of squares: 12"

67

The Delaware & Allegheny Railroad

Five scale miles of heavy-duty mainline railroading in N scale, one scene at a time

SQUARE-WISE, this is the second largest track plan in this book — 12½ squares long by 7½ squares wide, to be built in a 14' x 21½' obstruction-free area that can be completely devoted to railroad. With over 100 turnouts, it's also among the most complex. Thanks to the compactness of N scale, the whole thing fits in one end of a 22'-wide basement. And, this pike concentrates on those things for which N is best noted: running long passenger and freight trains and accommodating hundreds of pieces of rolling stock, in and out of sight.

The theme of the Delaware and Allegheny is a heavy-duty, single-track, late steam era, mountain-crossing railroad like the Western Maryland or Clinchfield — but with the passenger traffic of the B & O's Chicago and St. Louis main lines combined. Why not — freedom to combine things that turn you on and make the best "model prototypes" is the essence of model railroading!

Spiral aisles; straighter track. It's a five-scale-mile trip from loop to loop of the D & A's main line, none of which

overlaps itself thanks to the liberal use of double-faced backdrops. As is usually the case where the area is big enough to allow a choice, a spiral aisle arrangement works out somewhat better than a parallel-lobed one. There is a higher ratio of straight to curved track, and even though any railroad crossing the Alleghenies will have a lot of curves, the D & A should still try to get over the summit in straightforward fashion. Wrapping a railroad up to fit into a basement generally results in way too many horseshoes, so the spiral (which in this case has about two complete circles less curvature than a back-and-forth arrangement would have) comes a little closer to reality.

Top priority for the D & A, though, is passenger train switching. This is respected by envisioning Confluence City as pretty much the counterpart of the B & O's Cumberland, Maryland, where the two lines from different western terminals come together. D & A's traffic isn't quite heavy enough to justify running separate trains through to the east, though, so its operating pattern typically consists of combining trains

on the way east and splitting them on the way back. With set-out diners, sleepers, and head-end cars to be shuffled, the double slip switches at both ends of the long platform tracks will be kept busy.

Yard and service facilities. While the station tracks are curved, both for appearance and to allow the freight and passenger areas of the terminal to share the spotlight by being located end-to-end rather than side-by-side, trackage at the ends of the platforms where coupling and uncoupling must take place is straight. The coach and head-end car yard ladder is also straight so a minimum of storage space will be lost in locating uncoupling ramps to work reliably under the long cars.

The D & A is accommodating itself to the diesel by building separate facilities at the west end of the Confluence City yards, leaving the steam engine terminal out front where the railfans can get a good look at its still-busy components.

Working in empties-in/loads-out arrangements for simulating open-top traffic patterns without having to actu-

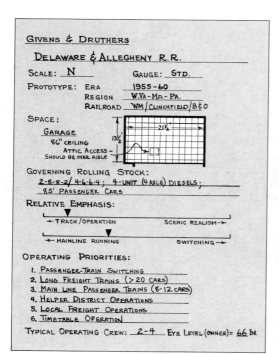

GIVENS & DRUTHERS

DELAWARE & ALLEGHENY R.R.

SCALE: N   GAUGE: STD.

PROTOTYPE: ERA 1955-60
REGION W. VA - MD - PA.
RAILROAD WM / CLINCHFIELD / B & O

SPACE:
GARAGE
86" CEILING
ATTIC ACCESS -
SHOULD BE OVER AISLE

GOVERNING ROLLING STOCK:
2-8-8-2 / 4-6-6-4; 4-UNIT (4 AXLE) DIESELS;
85' PASSENGER CARS

RELATIVE EMPHASIS:
← TRACK / OPERATION   SCENIC REALISM →
← MAINLINE RUNNING   SWITCHING →

OPERATING PRIORITIES:
1. PASSENGER-TRAIN SWITCHING
2. LONG FREIGHT TRAINS (> 20 CARS)
3. MAIN LINE PASSENGER TRAINS (8-12 CARS)
4. HELPER DISTRICT OPERATIONS
5. LOCAL FREIGHT OPERATIONS
6. TIMETABLE OPERATION

TYPICAL OPERATING CREW: 2-4   EYE LEVEL (OWNER) = 66 IN.

John Armstrong

The Delaware & Allegheny is a big railroad, big enough to feature one-scene-at-a-time scenic treatment. Passenger action similar to the B & O's operations at Cumberland, Maryland (opposite page) carries a high priority, and there's room for a photogenic sweeping curve such as this one at Photographer's Bend (above) on the author's O scale Canandaigua Southern Railroad.

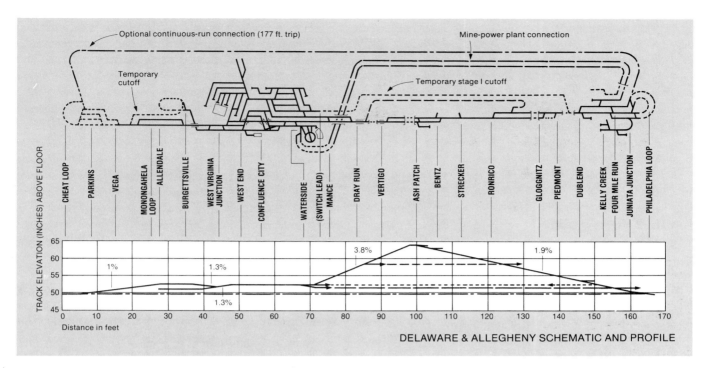

Optional continuous-run connection (177 ft. trip)   Mine-power plant connection

Temporary cutoff

Temporary stage I cutoff

TRACK ELEVATION (INCHES) ABOVE FLOOR

CHEAT LOOP
PARKINS
VEGA
MONONGAHELA LOOP
ALLENDALE
BURGETTSVILLE
WEST VIRGINIA JUNCTION
WEST END
CONFLUENCE CITY
WATERSIDE (SWITCH LEAD)
MANCE
DRAY RUN
VERTIGO
ASH PATCH
BENTZ
STRECKER
RONRICO
GLOGGNITZ
PIEDMONT
DUBLEND
KELLY CREEK
FOUR MILE RUN
JUNIATA JUNCTION
PHILADELPHIA LOOP

65
60
55
50
45

1%   1.3%   3.8%   1.9%

1.3%

0   10   20   30   40   50   60   70   80   90   100   110   120   130   140   150   160   170
Distance in feet

DELAWARE & ALLEGHENY SCHEMATIC AND PROFILE

ally load and unload the cars is no problem on a pike this big — in addition to the usual coal, how about wood-chip traffic in outsized hoppers or gondolas as well? Because there will still be a lot more coal traffic than can be accounted for by the mine and power plant in evidence on this segment of what is a far longer and busier railroad, the optional continuous-run connection to allow solid trains of minerals to run eastward and meet their westbound empty counterparts trip after trip is worth considering. At 5.4 scale miles per circuit, these runs will keep a lot of rolling stock gainfully employed.

A single-track grade. The D & A's

Allegheny crossing is east of the junction between its Cheat and Monongahela lines, so traffic up its Ash Patch grade is dense; in fact, there would be ample justification (and, in N scale plenty of room) for double track all the way up and over. As drawn, the single-track bottleneck across Vertigo Trestle is the choice in the interest of making this bridge look even longer, higher, and more perilous than it would if double tracked, but a double/triple-track mountain crossing is still a good option.

As it is, we can't resist a segment of triple track from Four Mile Run to Juniata Junction for that big-time flavor. Bringing the five Philadelphia Loop

switches out into the open is not only in the interest of comfort and reliability but also allows layover by the really long trains for which this pike will become noted.

At the other end of the railroad, Parkins provides considerable layover capacity, though not nearly as much as could be useful. The slimness of N scale trains allows maintaining access to Parkins' turnouts by simply moving the top-level tracks through West Virginia Junction out toward the aisle and leaving them exposed from above, behind an embankment but in front of the backdrop.

Options. Also flexible is the location

Jim Bradley

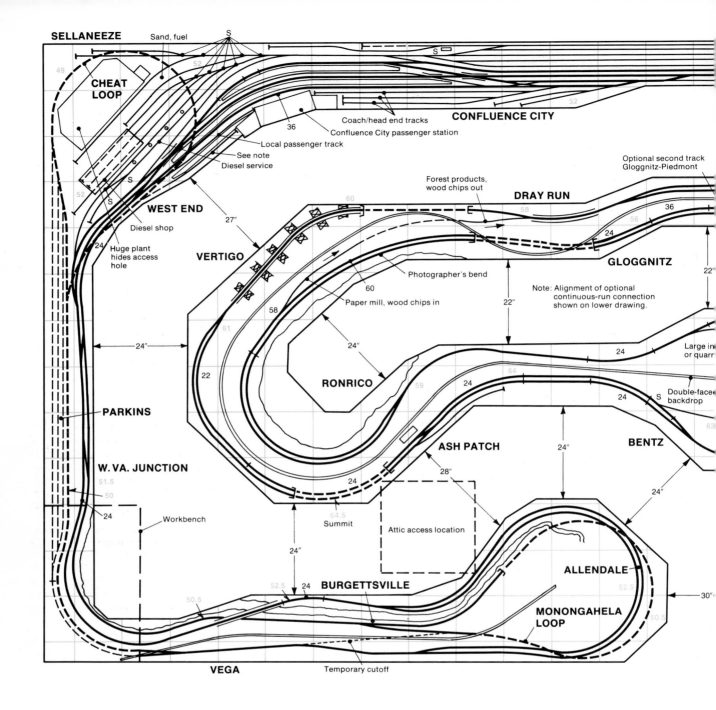

SELLANEEZE   Sand, fuel   S

49

CHEAT LOOP

52

CONFLUENCE CITY
S

Coach/head end tracks
Confluence City passenger station

Local passenger track
See note
Diesel service

52

36

52

WEST END

27"

Optional second track
Gloggnitz-Piedmont

Forest products,
wood chips out

DRAY RUN
60   58   36

VERTIGO
S

Diesel shop

24   Huge plant
hides access
hole

24

GLOGGNITZ

56

22"

Photographer's bend
60

58

Paper mill, wood chips in

22"

Note: Alignment of optional
continuous-run connection
shown on lower drawing.

61

24"

24"

Large in
or quarr

24"

PARKINS

RONRICO
59

24"

22

24"

Double-face
backdrop

24"

ASH PATCH
28"

BENTZ

64

24"

63

W. VA. JUNCTION

51.5

50

24

Workbench

64.5

Summit
24"

Attic access location

30"

ALLENDALE
52.5

52.5

24"

24"

MONONGAHELA
LOOP

50.5

52.5   24   BURGETTSVILLE
50.5

24"

VEGA   Temporary cutoff

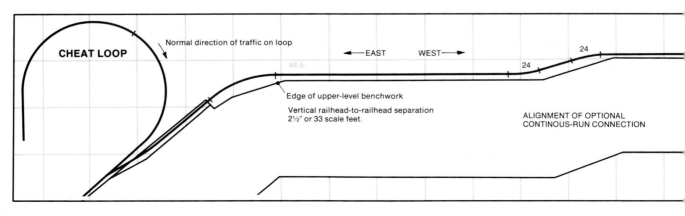

CHEAT LOOP

Normal direction of traffic on loop

EAST   WEST

24

49.5

24

Edge of upper-level benchwork

Vertical railhead-to-railhead separation
2½" or 33 scale feet.

ALIGNMENT OF OPTIONAL
CONTINOUS-RUN CONNECTION

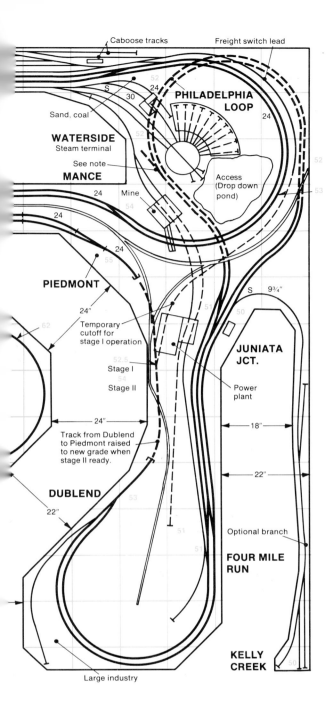

Caboose tracks
Freight switch lead

PHILADELPHIA
LOOP

52
S
30
24

WATERSIDE
Steam terminal

Sand, coal

See note

MANCE

52

Mine

Access
(Drop down
pond)

24
54

24

24

24

52

53

PIEDMONT

24"

Temporary
cutoff for
stage I operation

55

62

Stage I
Stage II

52.5

54

S
9¾"

50

JUNIATA
JCT.

Power
plant

24"

18"

Track from Dublend
to Piedmont raised
to new grade when
stage II ready.

22"

DUBLEND

22"

53

Optional branch

51

FOUR MILE
RUN

51

Large industry

KELLY
CREEK

50

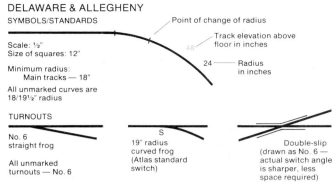

DELAWARE & ALLEGHENY
SYMBOLS/STANDARDS

Point of change of radius

Track elevation above
floor in inches

48

24 — Radius
in inches

Scale: ½"
Size of squares: 12"

Minimum radius:
   Main tracks — 18"
All unmarked curves are
18/19½" radius

TURNOUTS

No. 6
straight frog

S
19" radius
curved frog
(Atlas standard
switch)

Double-slip
(drawn as No. 6 —
actual switch angle
is sharper, less
space required)

All unmarked
turnouts — No. 6

TRACK CENTER SPACING

Tangent: 1¼" minimum — shown as 1⅓" (approximately)
Curves: shown as 1½" — actual spacing to be determined by test
   or set at 1⅜" minimum

of the Ash Patch summit. For the same reasons discussed in connection with the Durango, Ophir, & Northern plan the grades have been made highly asymmetrical, but they could be equalized to make both directions pusher grades or even to make the westbound climb the tough one.

As befits a pike of this complexity, construction in stages has been provided for, with temporary connections allowing a lot of railroading action before commencing some of the more complex and space-clogging construction required to bring the grand design to completion.

As a final challenge, note that the arrangement of exposed and hidden tracks at the Juniata Junction power plant is such that it's possible — with well-coordinated hands on two throttles — to simulate unloading-in-motion operations as strings of hopper cars crawl through the covered car-dumper section of the building.

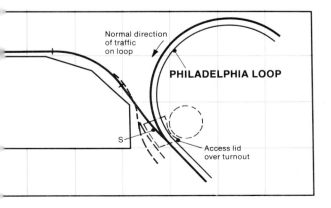

Normal direction
of traffic
on loop

PHILADELPHIA LOOP

S

Access lid
over turnout

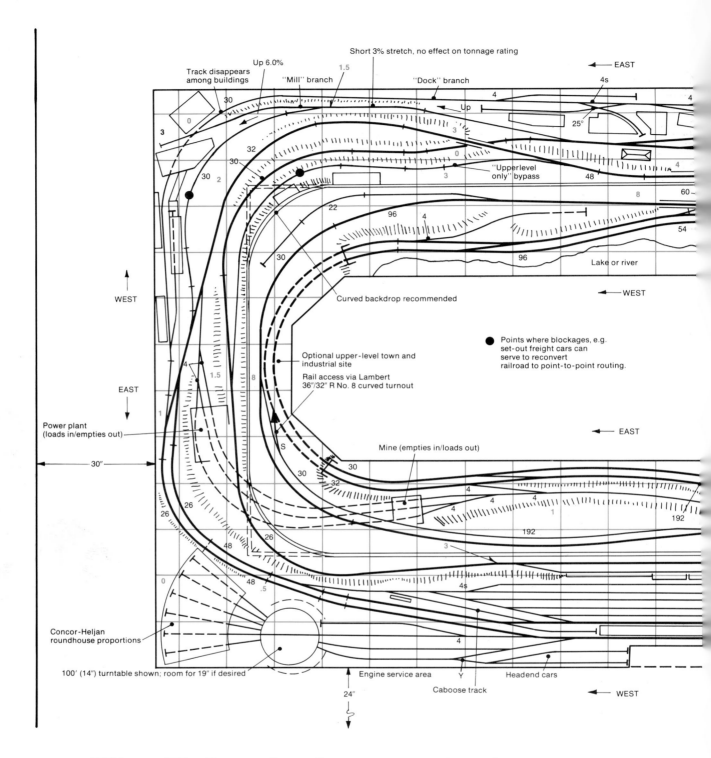

The Eclectic Central Railroad

A 13' x 24' HO island layout designed with sectional benchwork
so it can be dismantled, moved, and reassembled

THE TRAINS ARE the things that make model railroading fun, and there's no point in running trains that aren't to your liking just because they precisely fit a theme which can be represented within the layout conditions available. To some extent we are all collectors at heart, and the Eclectic Central's primary goal is to provide an attractive and practical place for a vast number and variety of trains to show themselves off doing their individual things.

With the proprietor of this layout variety isn't just a matter of mainline

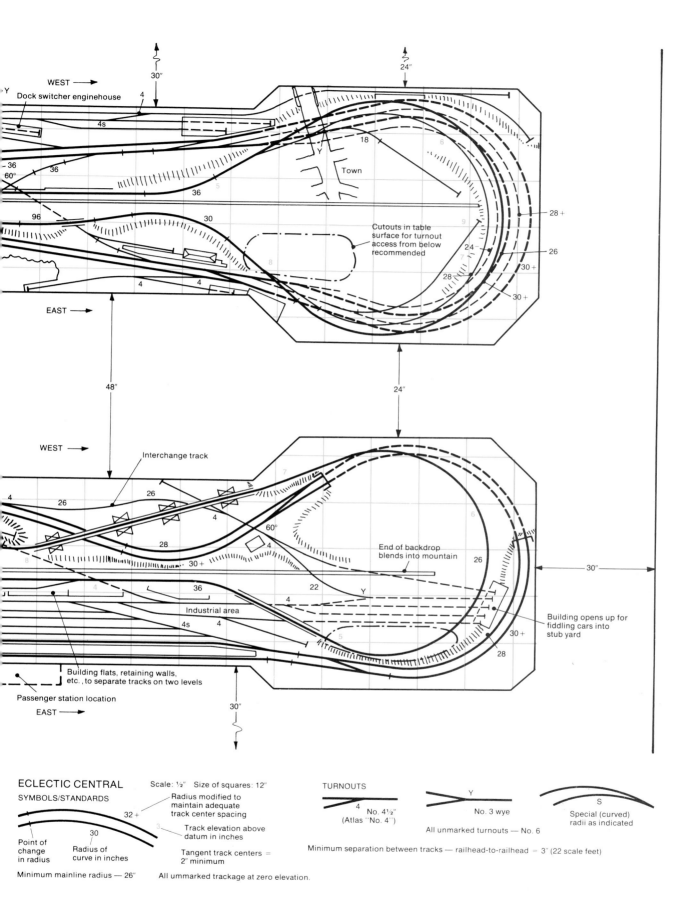

WEST →
Dock switcher enginehouse
4
30"
24"

Y
4s
36
60°
-36
96
30
Town
18
Y
6
28 +
Cutouts in table
surface for turnout
access from below
recommended
24
26
30 +
28
30 +
9
8
4
EAST →
48"
24"

WEST →
Interchange track
4
26
26
7
4
28
4
60°
End of backdrop
blends into mountain
26
30 +
8
36
22
Y
4
Industrial area
4s
4
5
Building opens up for
fiddling cars into
stub yard
30 +
28
Building flats, retaining walls,
etc., to separate tracks on two levels
Passenger station location
EAST →
30"
30"

ECLECTIC CENTRAL
SYMBOLS/STANDARDS

Scale: ½"   Size of squares: 12"
Radius modified to
maintain adequate
track center spacing
32 +
Track elevation above
datum in inches
30
Point of
change
in radius
Radius of
curve in inches
Tangent track centers =
2" minimum

Minimum mainline radius — 26"   All unmarked trackage at zero elevation.

TURNOUTS

4
No. 4½"
(Atlas "No. 4")

Y
No. 3 wye

S
Special (curved)
radii as indicated

All unmarked turnouts — No. 6

Minimum separation between tracks — railhead-to-railhead = 3" (22 scale feet)

running, either, because the local freight with its constantly varying consist rates a high priority too. But if the Baldwin freight Sharknoses in their NYC cigar-band livery happen to meet a veteran Ma & Pa Consolidation in the course of a run, that's okay too.

A railroad able to move. Furthermore, this railroad is to be an island pike, even though this means that it won't fill every nook and cranny of the 17' x 29' room currently available. The benchwork is to be built mostly in 4'-wide rectangular sections which can be moved and reassembled in a similar

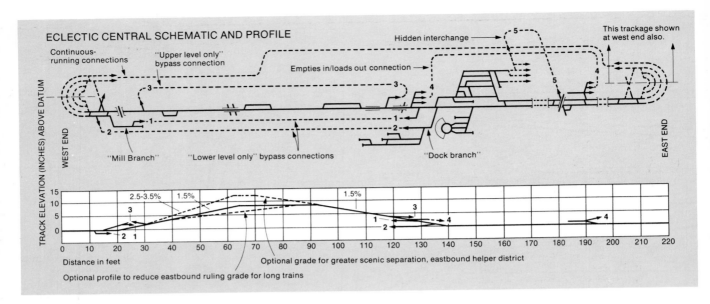

ECLECTIC CENTRAL SCHEMATIC AND PROFILE

Continuous-running connections

"Upper level only" bypass connection

Hidden interchange

This trackage shown at west end also.

Empties in/loads out connection

WEST END

EAST END

"Mill Branch"   "Lower level only" bypass connections   "Dock branch"

TRACK ELEVATION (INCHES) ABOVE DATUM

2.5-3.5%   1.5%   1.5%

Distance in feet

Optional profile to reduce eastbound ruling grade for long trains

Optional grade for greater scenic separation, eastbound helper district

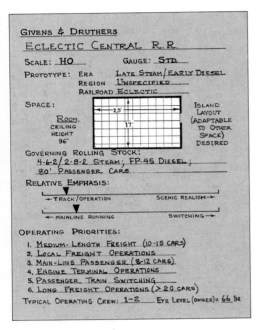

GIVENS & DRUTHERS

ECLECTIC CENTRAL R.R.

SCALE: HO   GAUGE: STD.

PROTOTYPE: ERA LATE STEAM / EARLY DIESEL
REGION UNSPECIFIED
RAILROAD ECLECTIC

SPACE:

ROOM,
CEILING
HEIGHT
96"

ISLAND
LAYOUT
(ADAPTABLE
TO OTHER
SPACE)
DESIRED

GOVERNING ROLLING STOCK:
4-6-2 / 2-8-2 STEAM; FP-45 DIESEL;
80' PASSENGER CARS

RELATIVE EMPHASIS:

←— TRACK / OPERATION   SCENIC REALISM —→

←— MAINLINE RUNNING   SWITCHING —→

OPERATING PRIORITIES:
1. MEDIUM-LENGTH FREIGHT (10-15 CARS)
2. LOCAL FREIGHT OPERATIONS
3. MAIN-LINE PASSENGER (8-12 CARS)
4. ENGINE TERMINAL OPERATIONS
5. PASSENGER TRAIN SWITCHING
6. LONG FREIGHT OPERATIONS (> 20 CARS)

TYPICAL OPERATING CREW: 1-2   EYE LEVEL (OWNER) = 66 IN.

but not identical area should a move be necessary during the lifetime of the layout.

As a result, although the railroad room is an uncluttered 6½ x 11 squares (considering that operation of the stiffest locomotives in the collection, Santa Fe 2-10-4s, is not expected and a 26" radius is acceptable), the area to be covered with tablework is more like 45

square squares when allowance is made for surrounding aisleways.

To this proprietor the sight of a second lap of track in the scene at any point is much less disturbing than having the same train orbiting at very high frequency, so the Eclectic Central is a twice-around horseshoe, 3.6 scale miles from end-loop to end-loop if it is operated in that fashion, or a similar distance around if a train takes the continuous-run route.

The sight of two trains passing nearby or over or under each other being even better to watch at times, the twice-around EC has some connections — they serve as industry spurs between times — which allow running simultaneously on upper- and lower-level ovals without interference. For solo operation, this means that there can be a lot of train-watching between moves in the yard or while shooting the breeze with visitors. At the same time, the continuous central backdrop avoids the shooting-gallery feeling.

The pool-table route. Grades are also optional. For those situations where a beautiful model — such as a diesel that trades ballast weight for a detailed and lighted interior — has severe tractive force limitations that keep it from hauling an appropriately long, good-looking consist over even a modest slope, the lower-level horseshoe provides a pool-table profile. The "moun-

tain" division of the upper level has room to reach bridge-crossing elevations via modest grades. Better scenic effects, of course, will result with steeper slopes, and a helper-district 2.5 percent or 3.5 percent in one direction can still be achieved while allowing long consists to run unassisted if headed the other way.

The "calks" of the horseshoe have been widened beyond the 4' limit. Although this means that these end segments of benchwork should be framed as two narrower sections to avoid any question of portability, the resulting short segments of 24" aisleway are not barriers to free circulation of operators and visitors. A strong point of the broader aisles elsewhere is the farther-back viewpoints they will afford.

Storage capacity. On the lower level of one of the calks there is room for some modest layover trackage of mostly standard-or-better curvature. Overall, there isn't going to be enough track to keep all those favorite trains on the railroad without clogging things up hopelessly, so a couple of the interchange-track and industrial-spur connections that help keep the local freights and switchers busy are arranged to allow some subtlety in fiddling cars on and off the pike. Every nice train deserves the chance to be heard clicking over a crossing, so some of those have been worked into the plan, too.

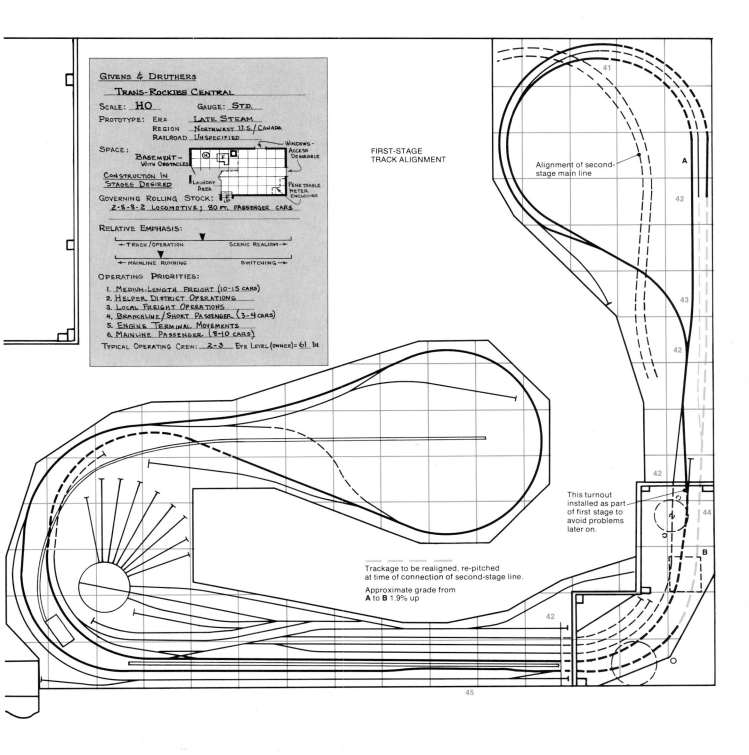

GIVENS & DRUTHERS

TRANS-ROCKIES CENTRAL

SCALE: **HO**   GAUGE: **STD.**

PROTOTYPE: ERA   LATE STEAM
      REGION   NORTHWEST U.S./CANADA
      RAILROAD   UNSPECIFIED

SPACE:
      BASEMENT—
      WITH OBSTACLES.

CONSTRUCTION IN
STAGES DESIRED

    WINDOWS—
    ACCESS
    DESIRABLE

    LAUNDRY
    AREA

    PENETRABLE
    METER
    ENCLOSURE

GOVERNING ROLLING STOCK:
2-8-8-2 LOCOMOTIVE; 80 FT. PASSENGER CARS

RELATIVE EMPHASIS:

←—TRACK/OPERATION   SCENIC REALISM—→

←—MAINLINE RUNNING   SWITCHING—→

OPERATING PRIORITIES:
1. MEDIUM-LENGTH FREIGHT (10-15 CARS)
2. HELPER DISTRICT OPERATIONS
3. LOCAL FREIGHT OPERATIONS
4. BRANCHLINE/SHORT PASSENGER (3-4 CARS)
5. ENGINE TERMINAL MOVEMENTS
6. MAINLINE PASSENGER (8-10 CARS)

TYPICAL OPERATING CREW: 2-3   EYE LEVEL (OWNER)= 61 IN.

FIRST-STAGE
TRACK ALIGNMENT

Alignment of second-
stage main line

A

42

43

42

This turnout
installed as part
of first stage to
avoid problems
later on.

42

44

B

Trackage to be realigned, re-pitched
at time of connection of second-stage line.

Approximate grade from
A to **B** 1.9% up

41

42

45

The Trans-Rockies Central Railroad

An HO layout pushed through, behind, and around formidable obstacles,
and designed for territorial expansion as more space becomes available

THE TRANS-ROCKIES CENTRAL, a free-lance railroad of the late-steam era set in mountainous Canadian Pacific/Great Northern/Northern Pacific territory, is planned from the beginning for two distinct stages of construction. Initially, enough space in the basement family room is to be held off limits to railroading to serve as a play area for the younger members and to accommodate some of their bulkier gear. In due course, the railroad can
push into this territory and even go on to the challenges of penetrating the utility area beyond.

The first stage — and first obstacles. Intended to provide some mainline running along with full operation

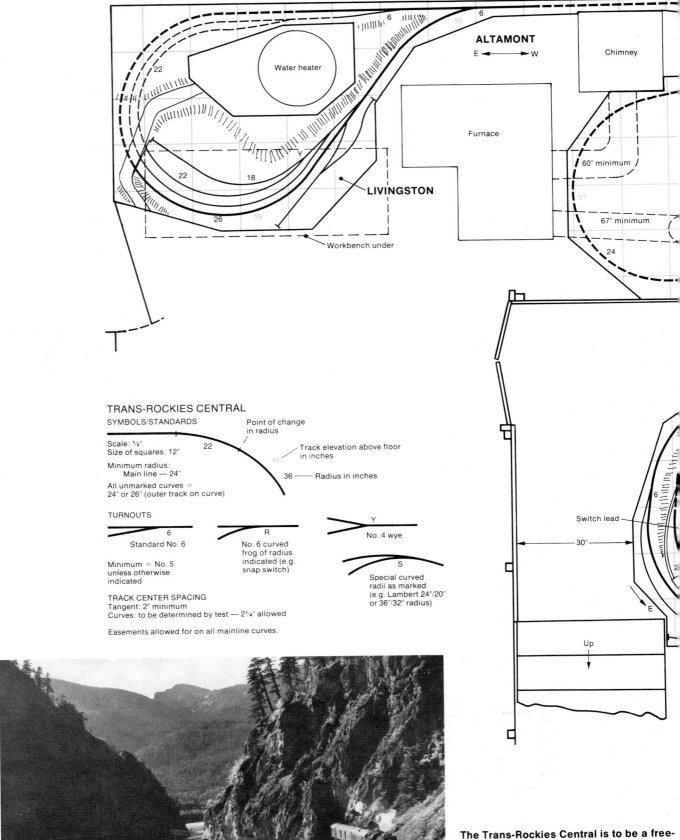

ALTAMONT

E ◄——► W

Chimney

Water heater

22

LIVINGSTON

Furnace

60" minimum

22   18

67" minimum

26   59

24

Y

Workbench under

TRANS-ROCKIES CENTRAL

SYMBOLS/STANDARDS

Point of change
in radius

22

Track elevation above floor
in inches

Scale: ½"
Size of squares: 12"

36 — Radius in inches

Minimum radius:
Main line — 24"

All unmarked curves =
24" or 26" (outer track on curve)

TURNOUTS

6
Standard No. 6

Minimum = No. 5
unless otherwise
indicated

R
No. 6 curved
frog of radius
indicated (e.g.
snap switch)

Y
No. 4 wye

S
Special curved
radii as marked
(e.g. Lambert 24"/20"
or 36"/32" radius)

TRACK CENTER SPACING
Tangent: 2" minimum
Curves: to be determined by test — 2¼" allowed

Easements allowed for on all mainline curves.

Switch lead

30"

E

Up

Canadian Pacific

The Trans-Rockies Central is to be a free-lance railroad, but it will draw heavily from Canadian Pacific's rugged crossing of the Rockies for its scenery. (Left) A CP passenger train in the Fraser River Canyon in British Columbia, and (right) a pair of photos showing the same freight train negotiating Tunnel No. 2 of CP's famed Spiral Tunnels in Kicking Horse Pass.

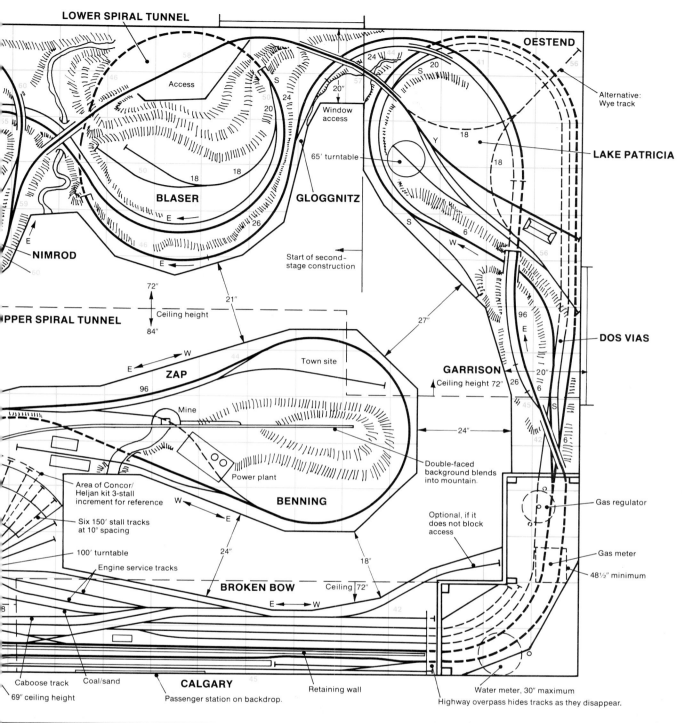

LOWER SPIRAL TUNNEL

OESTEND

Access

Alternative: Wye track

Window access

24

20

20"

LAKE PATRICIA

S

24

20

65' turntable

Y

18

18

BLASER

GLOGGNITZ

E

NIMROD

E

E

26

Start of second-stage construction

S

6

W

E

S

DOS VIAS

PPER SPIRAL TUNNEL

72"

Ceiling height

84"

21"

27"

96

E

20"

6

W

ZAP

Town site

GARRISON

E

96

Ceiling height 72"

26

S

Mine

24"

Power plant

Double-faced background blends into mountain.

Area of Concor/ Heljan kit 3-stall increment for reference

BENNING

W

E

Gas regulator

Six 150' stall tracks at 10° spacing

100' turntable

Engine service tracks

24"

18

Optional, if it does not block access

Gas meter

48½" minimum

BROKEN BOW

Ceiling 72"

Caboose track

Coal/sand

CALGARY

E

W

Retaining wall

Water meter, 30" maximum

69" ceiling height

Passenger station on backdrop.

Highway overpass hides tracks as they disappear.

Both photos, Fred Stoes

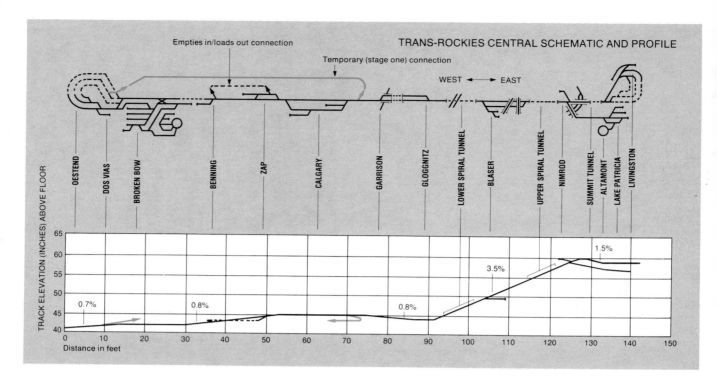

of the pike's major yard, the 14' x 15' first stage is essentially a dogbone with the two sides of its shank treated as separate portions of a single-track main line. Experience in overcoming obstacles which will come in handy later is to be acquired in fitting several tracks through a paneled enclosure hiding the squatty water heater and the overhead gas meter and regulator; between them they determine the height of the railroad.

Calgary is a separate station, schematically quite a distance from the division-point yards at Broken Bow, so it is raised 3" (22 scale feet) above its neighbor. A stretch of retaining wall emphasizes the separation without taking up any space.

In anticipation of second-stage construction, a turnout that for the time being goes nowhere is shown over the gas regulator in the lower right corner. Its points are far enough removed from the paneling above it to permit any troubleshooting that might be necessary during operation of the completed railroad, but the switch would be a stinker to install during the repitching and reconnecting process that will precede the opening of the pike's "Eastern Extension" through the Rockies.

More obstacles. Engineering a practical path through the toils of the furnace-chimney connection while starting from the level dictated by the gas appliances and leaving acceptable access for opening windows occasionally is at least as severe a challenge as that faced by the Canadian Pacific in Kicking Horse Pass. The answer is the

same — two spiral tunnels. With them, the grade on the Big Hill is kept to 3.5 percent, which is a good model representation of the prototype's 2.2 percent so far as justifying helper engines and providing impressively vertical scenery is concerned. The deep scene extending back more than four feet from a "viewing notch" between Nimrod and Blaser will be impressive; the beneath-mountain access from the rear makes it practical.

Curves are necessarily limited to conventional standards (24") at many points on the main line. This will cause no operating problems for the 2-8-8-2s which the Trans-Rockies will use to conquer the grades, but the matter of clearance between tracks has to be considered when that boiler front swings out into space. Tests before the track goes down are essential; from an appearance standpoint, as little widening as is necessary to let the full-length passenger cars clear the articulated's running boards on the passing tracks is desirable. Cutting it too close would be worse, because the S-curved route won't always allow the dispatcher to keep the 2-8-8-2s on the outside track all the way.

A bit of backtracking. As is typical for a railroad of this size where the emphasis is on mainline operations with fairly long runs, walk-around access is provided to all points. It is necessary to backtrack a bit at one point (between Zap and Calgary) to follow a train over the entire route, and this means that the generally desirable situation of always having west to the left, east to the

right as you face any segment of main line cannot be maintained.

We have chosen to have the most important sections of line (those through Broken Bow and on east through Zap) follow the rule. Once you get in the Spiral Tunnel territory — as you are particularly aware if you've tried to orient yourself there in the Canadian Rockies as a train works its way through the maze — things are going to be so confusing that whether the train is heading east or west doesn't matter!

The Lake Patricia branch. Yet a third stage of construction is provided by the Lake Patricia branch, a passenger-oriented spur taking Pullman passengers from the East directly to their resort. Since this line is hooked on backwards so far as the principal direction of traffic flow is concerned, the operating department will have to consider several options in handling the through passenger cars, all of them interesting from a railfan standpoint even if they would be of varying degrees of attractiveness economically to a prototype railroad.

To make the best use of the space, this railroad has been designed to use No. 5 turnouts at most points, which means they will have to be built by hand if using commercially available prefabricated ones in other sizes. Considering the 24" mainline curvature, No. 4½s (Atlas "No. 4s") would be a satisfactory substitute in most cases. At some points in the plan the space saving of curved turnouts is essential; fortunately, those shown are now commercially available.

Index

Easy-to-Build
ELECTRONIC PROJE
for Model Railroader

NEW HANOVER COUNTY PUBLIC LIBRARY
3 4200 00195 7362

A SPECIAL REPRINT FROM **Model Railroader** MAGAZINE $6.50

CTC-16e

A model railroad command
control system you can build

BY KEITH GUTIERREZ

BY PETER J. THORNE

All the information you
need to build your own
electronic devices, from
which machine power
supplies to steam and
diesel sound systems.

**HOW TO REPAIR
COMMERCIAL
THROTTLES**

Including parts lists,
schematics, and step-
by-step instructions.

Build your own
WALKAROUND
THROTTLE!

The ideal book for beginners!

THE **abc's** OF
from the pages of **Model Railroader**
MODEL
RAILROADING

23 chapters to help you get
started in model railroading

SCENERY
FOR MODEL RAILROADS

BY BILL McCLANAHAN

REVISED
EDITION
INCLUDING
HARD-SHELL
SCENERY
AND
ZIP
TEXTURING

HOW THE EXPERTS DO IT
MADE EASY FOR BEGINNERS

how to
WIRE
your
model
railroad

Including Wiring for Sectional Track

BY LINN H. WESTCOTT

WIRING made
simple and clear
for everyone

HO RAILROAD
that grows
By Linn H. Westcott

8
easy
steps

Start on a sheet of

Including Bridges,
Scenery, and Wiring

ALL NEW
FUN FOR THE ENTIRE FAMILY
**small railroads
YOU can build**
EDITED BY BOB HAYDEN

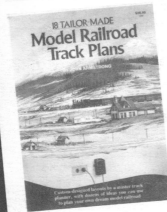

Proven Methods Plus NEW Ideas for Scenery, Wiring, Operation

From Complete Lists of Materials... to Finished Layouts

from
**model
railroader**
HO Narrow Gauge
Railroad You Can Build
BY MALCOLM FURLOW

SAN JUAN
CENTRAL

How to build the San Juan Central
an 8 x 10 HOn3 layout that features
sectional construction and new
lightweight scenery techniques.

N Scale Primer
A BEGINNER'S GUIDE TO N SCALE MODEL RAILROADING
BY RUSS LARSON

TRACK PLANS
FOR SECTIONAL
TRACK

By Linn Westcott
144
TRACK PLANS
including lists of pieces needed
for rug, table and custom layouts

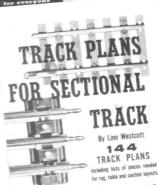

HO, 0-27, S and O gauges

18 TAILOR-MADE
**Model Railroad
Track Plans**
BY ARMSTRONG

Custom-designed layouts by a master track
planner, with dozens of ideas you can use
to plan your own dream model railroad

101
TRACK PLANS

A HANDBOOK FOR MODEL RAILROADERS AND RAILFANS
TRACK PLANNING
for realistic operation
BY JOHN ARMSTRONG

REVISED
AND
UPDATED

3373   3373

How prototype railroads are
designed to operate
How you can design
your model railroad

NEW HANOVER COUNTY PUBLIC LIBRARY
201 CHESTNUT ST.
WILMINGTON, NC   28401

NLib